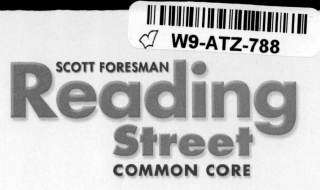

SCOTT FORESMAN

Reading Street
COMMON CORE

Reading Street Common Core
Writing to Sources

Glenview, Illinois

Boston, Massachusetts

Chandler, Arizona

Upper Saddle River, New Jersey

ALWAYS LEARNING   PEARSON

ISBN-13: 978-0-328-76859-2
ISBN-10:　　0-328-76859-6
5 6 7 8 9 10　V0N4　16 15 14 13

Reading Street Common Core
Writing to Sources

Reading Street Common Core Writing to Sources makes fact-finding fun! Students substantiate their claims and communicate in writing what they have learned from one text and then from other related texts.

Reading Street Common Core Writing to Sources encourages students to collaborate and share their growing knowledge with peers, adding quality experiences in the art of using text-based evidence.

Reading Street Common Core Writing to Sources provides more practice with all modes of writing—argument, informative/explanatory, and narrative—and connects to the Common Core State Standards.

Reading Street Common Core Writing to Sources gives students opportunities to complete Performance Tasks by writing in response to what they read and collaborating with others.

Reading Street Common Core Writing to Sources offers you an alternative approach to writing tasks on Reading Street!

1 Write Like a Reporter
Write to one source.
Students respond to the main selection by citing evidence from the text.

2 Connect the Texts
Write to two sources.
Students respond to the main and paired selections by citing evidence from the texts.

3 Prove It! Unit Writing Task
Write to multiple sources.
Students analyze multiple sources within a unit and cite evidence from the texts.

4 More Connect the Texts
Additional lessons specific to writing forms within all modes of writing—argument, informative/explanatory, and narrative—are included.

"Write Like a Reporter!"

Table of Contents

Get Ready for Performance Tasks

Table of Contents

More Connect the Texts — 197

Writing Forms

Unit 1 Meeting Challenges

Writing Focus: Informative/Explanatory

Write Like a Reporter
Informative/Explanatory Paragraph

Student Prompt Reread the section on pp. 34–38 and summarize how Brady tries to keep Ben alive. Write a paragraph with precise language to explain how Brady responds to this challenge and how the use of first-person point of view influences the description of events. Support your conclusions with examples from the text, including facts and concrete details.

_____

_____

_____

_____

_____

_____

_____

_____

_____

_____

_____

_____

_____

_____

_____

_____

_____

_____

Write Like a Reporter

Informative/Explanatory Paragraph

> **Student Prompt, p. 6** Reread the section on pp. 34–38 and summarize how Brady tries to keep Ben alive. Write a paragraph with precise language to explain how Brady responds to this challenge and how the use of first-person point of view influences the description of events. Support your conclusions with examples from the text, including facts and concrete details.

Writing to Sources Before students begin their explanatory paragraphs, have them summarize the part of the story in which Brady is fighting to save Ben's life. In their explanations, students should use concrete words, phrases, and details from the text to help explain Brady's responses to this life-and-death challenge. Students should then clarify how the first-person point of view adds to the urgency and drama of the story. Remind students to reread the text carefully and base their responses on details from the original story.

Students' paragraphs should:

- clearly describe how point of view influences the description of events
- develop the topic with facts and concrete details from the text
- use precise language to explain the topic
- demonstrate strong command of the conventions of standard written English

---

ⓒ Common Core State Standards

Writing 2. Write informative/explanatory texts to examine a topic and convey ideas and information clearly. **Writing 9.a.** Apply grade 5 Reading standards to literature (e.g., "Compare and contrast two or more characters, settings, or events in a story or a drama, drawing on specific details in the text [e.g., how characters interact]").

Connect the Texts

Informative/Explanatory Essay

> **Student Prompt** Look back at *Red Kayak* and "What Will I Do in an Emergency?" How do the instructions in the how-to text differ from those Brady uses to revive Ben? How are they similar? Write a short essay that compares and contrasts the information in "What Will I Do in an Emergency?" with the ABC method Brady uses in *Red Kayak*. Carefully reread both texts to find facts, concrete details, and quotations to support your explanation.

_____

_____

_____

_____

_____

_____

_____

_____

_____

_____

_____

_____

_____

_____

_____

_____

_____

_____

Connect the Texts
Informative/Explanatory Essay

Student Prompt, p. 8 Look back at *Red Kayak* and "What Will I Do in an Emergency?" How do the instructions in the how-to text differ from those Brady uses to revive Ben? How are they similar? Write a short essay that compares and contrasts the information in "What Will I Do in an Emergency?" with the ABC method Brady uses in *Red Kayak*. Carefully reread both texts to find facts, concrete details, and quotations to support your explanation.

Writing to Sources Discuss with students how *Red Kayak* and "What Will I Do in an Emergency?" present different options of what to do in an emergency. Then have them carefully reread the story and the how-to text to find specific facts and details to compare and contrast. Have students look at the organizational structure the authors use to convey information in the texts. Students' paragraphs should include quotations, concrete details, and facts from both texts to support their conclusions.

Informative/Explanatory Writing Rubric

Score	Focus	Organization	Development of Evidence	Language and Vocabulary	Conventions
4	Main idea is clearly conveyed and well supported; response is focused.	Organization is clear and effective, creating a sense of cohesion.	Evidence is relevant and thorough; includes facts and details.	Ideas are clearly and effectively conveyed, using precise language and/or domain-specific vocabulary.	Command of conventions is strongly demonstrated.
3	Main idea is clear, adequately supported; response is generally focused.	Organization is clear, though minor flaws may be present and some ideas may be disconnected.	Evidence is adequate and includes facts and details.	Ideas are adequately conveyed, using both precise and more general language; may include domain-specific vocabulary.	Command of conventions is sufficiently demonstrated.
2	Main idea is somewhat supported; lacks focus or includes unnecessary material.	Organization is inconsistent, and flaws are apparent.	Evidence is uneven or incomplete; insufficient use of facts and details.	Ideas are unevenly conveyed, using overly-simplistic language; lacks domain-specific vocabulary.	Command of conventions is uneven.
1	Response may be confusing, unfocused; main idea insufficiently supported.	Organization is poor or nonexistent.	Evidence is poor or nonexistent.	Ideas are conveyed in a vague, unclear, or confusing manner.	There is very little command of conventions.
0	The response shows no evidence of the ability to construct a coherent explanatory essay using information from sources.				

© Common Core State Standards

Writing 2. Write informative/explanatory texts to examine a topic and convey ideas and information clearly. **Writing 9.a.** Apply grade 5 Reading standards to literature (e.g., "Compare and contrast two or more characters, settings, or events in a story or a drama, drawing on specific details in the text [e.g., how characters interact]"). **Writing 9.b.** Apply grade 5 Reading standards to informational texts (e.g., "Explain how an author uses reasons and evidence to support particular points in a text, identifying which reasons and evidence support which point[s]").

Write Like a Reporter
Informative/Explanatory Paragraph

Student Prompt Reread the section on pp. 63–73 and summarize Thunder Rose's adventures with the longhorn herd and the tornadoes. Create a list of metaphors and similes. Then write a one-paragraph explanation of what three or four of these metaphors and similes mean. Use domain-specific vocabulary to explain how the figurative language adds to the tall tale's meaning and tone. Support your explanation with specific examples from the text, including quotations.

_____

_____

_____

_____

_____

_____

_____

_____

_____

_____

_____

_____

_____

_____

_____

_____

Write Like a Reporter

Informative/Explanatory Paragraph

Student Prompt, p. 10 Reread the section on pp. 63–73 and summarize Thunder Rose's adventures with the longhorn herd and the tornadoes. Create a list of metaphors and similes. Then write a one-paragraph explanation of what three or four of these metaphors and similes mean. Use domain-specific vocabulary to explain how the figurative language adds to the tall tale's meaning and tone. Support your explanation with specific examples from the text, including quotations.

Writing to Sources As students reread the passage, have them list each metaphor and simile. Remind them that metaphors and similes are examples of figurative language. In their explanations, students should clearly define and explain their chosen metaphors and similes using domain-specific vocabulary. Ask them to consider how figurative language contributes to the author's meaning and tone. Remind students to reread the text carefully and base their explanations on details from the original story.

Students' paragraphs should:

- clearly identify and explain metaphors and similes
- develop the topic with quotations and other examples from the text
- use domain-specific vocabulary to explain the topic
- demonstrate strong command of the conventions of standard written English

---

ⓒ Common Core State Standards

Writing 2. Write informative/explanatory texts to examine a topic and convey ideas and information clearly. **Writing 9.a.** Apply grade 5 Reading standards to literature (e.g., "Compare and contrast two or more characters, settings, or events in a story or a drama, drawing on specific details in the text [e.g., how characters interact]").

Connect the Texts

Informative/Explanatory Essay

Student Prompt Look back at *Thunder Rose* and "Measuring Tornadoes." Using the Fujita scale, decide both the rating and the damage level of the tornadoes described in *Thunder Rose*. Then write a short essay that explains your choices. Carefully reread both texts to find facts, concrete details, and accurate quotations to support your explanation.

_____

_____

_____

_____

_____

_____

_____

_____

_____

_____

_____

_____

_____

_____

_____

_____

Connect the Texts
Informative/Explanatory Essay

Student Prompt, p. 12 Look back at *Thunder Rose* and "Measuring Tornadoes." Using the Fujita scale, decide both the rating and the damage level of the tornadoes described in *Thunder Rose*. Then write a short essay that explains your choices. Carefully reread both texts to find facts, concrete details, and accurate quotations to support your explanation.

Writing to Sources Discuss with students how to apply the Fujita scale from "Measuring Tornadoes" to the fictitious tornadoes in *Thunder Rose*. Then have them carefully reread the story and the expository text to find specific facts and details. Remind them to include accurate quotations, concrete details, and facts to support their explanations.

	Informative/Explanatory Writing Rubric				
Score	Focus	Organization	Development of Evidence	Language and Vocabulary	Conventions
4	Main idea is clearly conveyed and well supported; response is focused.	Organization is clear and effective, creating a sense of cohesion.	Evidence is relevant and thorough; includes facts and details.	Ideas are clearly and effectively conveyed, using precise language and/or domain-specific vocabulary.	Command of conventions is strongly demonstrated.
3	Main idea is clear, adequately supported; response is generally focused.	Organization is clear, though minor flaws may be present and some ideas may be disconnected.	Evidence is adequate and includes facts and details.	Ideas are adequately conveyed, using both precise and more general language; may include domain-specific vocabulary.	Command of conventions is sufficiently demonstrated.
2	Main idea is somewhat supported; lacks focus or includes unnecessary material.	Organization is inconsistent, and flaws are apparent.	Evidence is uneven or incomplete; insufficient use of facts and details.	Ideas are unevenly conveyed, using overly-simplistic language; lacks domain-specific vocabulary.	Command of conventions is uneven.
1	Response may be confusing, unfocused; main idea insufficiently supported.	Organization is poor or nonexistent.	Evidence is poor or nonexistent.	Ideas are conveyed in a vague, unclear, or confusing manner.	There is very little command of conventions.
0	The response shows no evidence of the ability to construct a coherent explanatory essay using information from sources.				

Ⓒ **Common Core State Standards**

Writing 2. Write informative/explanatory texts to examine a topic and convey ideas and information clearly. **Writing 9.a.** Apply grade 5 Reading standards to literature (e.g., "Compare and contrast two or more characters, settings, or events in a story or a drama, drawing on specific details in the text [e.g., how characters interact]"). **Writing 9.b.** Apply grade 5 Reading standards to informational texts (e.g., "Explain how an author uses reasons and evidence to support particular points in a text, identifying which reasons and evidence support which point[s]").

Write Like a Reporter
Informative/Explanatory Paragraph

Student Prompt Reread the section on pp. 94–97 and summarize the process Karana uses to build a fence. Create a list of the steps in chronological order. Then write a paragraph that explains how she creates the fence. Include transitions, such as *first, next,* and *then,* to show the chronology of events. Also include descriptions and details based on the original text in your explanation.

_____

_____

_____

_____

_____

_____

_____

_____

_____

_____

_____

_____

_____

_____

_____

Write Like a Reporter

Informative/Explanatory Paragraph

> **Student Prompt, p. 14** Reread the section on pp. 94–97 and summarize the process Karana uses to build a fence. Create a list of the steps in chronological order. Then write a paragraph that explains how she creates the fence. Include transitions, such as *first, next,* and *then,* to show the chronology of events. Also include descriptions and details based on the original text in your explanation.

Writing to Sources As students reread the section, have them list each step of Karana's fence building in order. Before they begin writing, remind them that the chronology of events in their explanations must remain the same as in the story. Remind them to use transitions to make the order clear. They should also include facts and details to develop the explanation. Remind students to reread the text carefully and base their explanations on details from the original story.

Students' paragraphs should:

- clearly state the proper chronological order of events in the text
- develop the topic with facts and details from the text
- link ideas with words such as *first, next,* and *then*
- demonstrate strong command of the conventions of standard written English

Ⓒ **Common Core State Standards**

Writing 2. Write informative/explanatory texts to examine a topic and convey ideas and information clearly. **Writing 9.a.** Apply grade 5 Reading standards to literature (e.g., "Compare and contrast two or more characters, settings, or events in a story or a drama, drawing on specific details in the text [e.g., how characters interact]").

Connect the Texts
Informative/Explanatory Essay

Student Prompt Look back at *Island of the Blue Dolphins* and "Seven Survival Questions." Did Karana follow any of the survival information given under the question "What makes a place safe?" In a short explanatory essay, clarify whether Karana uses any of this advice as she builds her home. Carefully reread both texts to find facts, concrete details, and accurate quotations to support your explanation.

_____

_____

_____

_____

_____

_____

_____

_____

_____

_____

_____

_____

_____

_____

_____

_____

_____

_____

Connect the Texts

Informative/Explanatory Essay

Student Prompt, p. 16 Look back at *Island of the Blue Dolphins* and "Seven Survival Questions." Did Karana follow any of the survival information under the question "What makes a place safe?" In a short explanatory essay, clarify if Karana uses any of this advice as she builds her home. Carefully reread both texts to find facts, concrete details, and accurate quotations to support your explanation.

Writing to Sources Discuss with students whether Karana of *Island of the Blue Dolphins* applies any of the survival skills from "Seven Survival Questions" when building a house on a deserted island. Have students clarify their explanations carefully with information drawn from both texts. Students' paragraphs should include accurate quotations, concrete details, and facts to support their conclusions.

Score	Focus	Organization	Development of Evidence	Language and Vocabulary	Conventions
Informative/Explanatory Writing Rubric					
4	Main idea is clearly conveyed and well supported; response is focused.	Organization is clear and effective, creating a sense of cohesion.	Evidence is relevant and thorough; includes facts and details.	Ideas are clearly and effectively conveyed, using precise language and/or domain-specific vocabulary.	Command of conventions is strongly demonstrated.
3	Main idea is clear, adequately supported; response is generally focused.	Organization is clear, though minor flaws may be present and some ideas may be disconnected.	Evidence is adequate and includes facts and details.	Ideas are adequately conveyed, using both precise and more general language; may include domain-specific vocabulary.	Command of conventions is sufficiently demonstrated.
2	Main idea is somewhat supported; lacks focus or includes unnecessary material.	Organization is inconsistent, and flaws are apparent.	Evidence is uneven or incomplete; insufficient use of facts and details.	Ideas are unevenly conveyed, using overly-simplistic language; lacks domain-specific vocabulary.	Command of conventions is uneven.
1	Response may be confusing, unfocused; main idea insufficiently supported.	Organization is poor or nonexistent.	Evidence is poor or nonexistent.	Ideas are conveyed in a vague, unclear, or confusing manner.	There is very little command of conventions.
0	The response shows no evidence of the ability to construct a coherent explanatory essay using information from sources.				

© Common Core State Standards

Writing 2. Write informative/explanatory texts to examine a topic and convey ideas and information clearly. **Writing 9.a.** Apply grade 5 Reading standards to literature (e.g., "Compare and contrast two or more characters, settings, or events in a story or a drama, drawing on specific details in the text [e.g., how characters interact]"). **Writing 9.b.** Apply grade 5 Reading standards to informational texts (e.g., "Explain how an author uses reasons and evidence to support particular points in a text, identifying which reasons and evidence support which point[s]").

Write Like a Reporter
Informative/Explanatory Paragraph

Student Prompt Reread the section on pp. 124–128 and summarize the sequence of events in which Satchel Paige and Josh Gibson face each other on the baseball field. Write a paragraph that examines the relationship between these individuals based on specific information from the text. Use domain-specific vocabulary to develop your explanation with examples from the text, including facts, concrete details, and accurate quotations.

_____

_____

_____

_____

_____

_____

_____

_____

_____

_____

_____

_____

_____

_____

_____

_____

_____

_____

Write Like a Reporter

Informative/Explanatory Paragraph

Student Prompt, p. 18 Reread the section on pp. 124–128 and summarize the sequence of events in which Satchel Paige and Josh Gibson face each other on the baseball field. Write a paragraph that examines the relationship between these individuals based on specific information from the text. Use domain-specific vocabulary to develop your explanation with examples from the text, including facts, concrete details, and accurate quotations.

Writing to Sources Before students begin their explanatory paragraphs, have them summarize this part of the story. Specifically, have them focus on when Satchel Paige pitches to Josh Gibson in the 1942 Negro World Series. In their explanations, students should use facts, concrete details, and accurate quotations from the text to explain the relationship between the two men. Remind students to reread the text carefully and base their responses on details from the original story.

Students' paragraphs should:

- clearly describe the relationship between two characters
- develop the topic with facts, concrete details, and quotations from the text
- use domain-specific vocabulary to explain the topic
- demonstrate strong command of the conventions of standard written English

© **Common Core State Standards**

Writing 2. Write informative/explanatory texts to examine a topic and convey ideas and information clearly. **Writing 9.b.** Apply grade 5 Reading standards to informational texts (e.g., "Explain how an author uses reasons and evidence to support particular points in a text, identifying which reasons and evidence support which point[s]").

Connect the Texts
Informative/Explanatory Essay

Student Prompt Look back at *Satchel Paige* and "Roberto Clemente." What do the two baseball players have in common? Write a short essay that compares and contrasts information in the biography of Clemente with the biographical information in *Satchel Paige*. Carefully reread both texts to find facts, concrete details, and accurate quotations to support your explanation.

_____

_____

_____

_____

_____

_____

_____

_____

_____

_____

_____

_____

_____

_____

_____

_____

_____

_____

_____

Connect the Texts
Informative/Explanatory Essay

Student Prompt, p. 20 Look back at *Satchel Paige* and "Roberto Clemente." What do the two baseball players have in common? Write a short essay that compares and contrasts information in the biography of Clemente with the biographical information in *Satchel Paige*. Carefully reread both texts to find facts, concrete details, and accurate quotations to support your explanation.

Writing to Sources Discuss with students how *Satchel Paige* and "Roberto Clemente" present the backgrounds and life experiences of two baseball players. Then have them carefully reread both biographies to find specific facts and details to compare and contrast. Students' responses should include accurate quotations, concrete details, and facts from the texts to support their conclusions.

		Informative/Explanatory Writing Rubric			
Score	Focus	Organization	Development of Evidence	Language and Vocabulary	Conventions
4	Main idea is clearly conveyed and well supported; response is focused.	Organization is clear and effective, creating a sense of cohesion.	Evidence is relevant and thorough; includes facts and details.	Ideas are clearly and effectively conveyed, using precise language and/or domain-specific vocabulary.	Command of conventions is strongly demonstrated.
3	Main idea is clear, adequately supported; response is generally focused.	Organization is clear, though minor flaws may be present and some ideas may be disconnected.	Evidence is adequate and includes facts and details.	Ideas are adequately conveyed, using both precise and more general language; may include domain-specific vocabulary.	Command of conventions is sufficiently demonstrated.
2	Main idea is somewhat supported; lacks focus or includes unnecessary material.	Organization is inconsistent, and flaws are apparent.	Evidence is uneven or incomplete; insufficient use of facts and details.	Ideas are unevenly conveyed, using overly-simplistic language; lacks domain-specific vocabulary.	Command of conventions is uneven.
1	Response may be confusing, unfocused; main idea insufficiently supported.	Organization is poor or nonexistent.	Evidence is poor or nonexistent.	Ideas are conveyed in a vague, unclear, or confusing manner.	There is very little command of conventions.
0	The response shows no evidence of the ability to construct a coherent explanatory essay using information from sources.				

Ⓒ **Common Core State Standards**

Writing 2. Write informative/explanatory texts to examine a topic and convey ideas and information clearly. **Writing 9.b.** Apply grade 5 Reading standards to informational texts (e.g., "Explain how an author uses reasons and evidence to support particular points in a text, identifying which reasons and evidence support which point[s]").

Write Like a Reporter
Informative/Explanatory Paragraph

Student Prompt Reread *Ten Mile Day* on pp. 146–159 and summarize the sequence of events. Take notes on how the illustrations correspond with different parts of the text. Then use precise language to write a one-paragraph explanation that focuses on how the illustrations clarify and contribute to the text's meaning and tone. Support your explanation with examples from the text, including specific facts, definitions, and concrete details.

_____

_____

_____

_____

_____

_____

_____

_____

_____

_____

_____

_____

_____

_____

_____

_____

Write Like a Reporter

Informative/Explanatory Paragraph

> **Student Prompt, p. 22** Reread *Ten Mile Day* on pp. 146–159 and summarize the sequence of events. Take notes on how the illustrations correspond with different parts of the text. Then use precise language to write a one-paragraph explanation that focuses on how the illustrations clarify and contribute to the text's meaning and tone. Support your explanation with examples from the text, including specific facts, definitions, and concrete details.

Writing to Sources As students reread *Ten Mile Day,* have them locate which specific parts of the text correspond with the illustrations. In their explanations, students should use concrete words, phrases, and details from the text to help explain what the illustrations depict and why those moments were illustrated. Students should then use precise language to analyze how the illustrations contribute to and clarify the text. Remind students to reread the text carefully and base their responses on details from the original story.

Students' paragraphs should:

- clearly explain how specific illustrations contribute to and clarify the text's meaning and tone
- develop the topic with specific facts, definitions, and concrete details from the text
- use precise language to describe the images and their contribution to the text
- demonstrate strong command of the conventions of standard written English

Ⓒ **Common Core State Standards**

Writing 2. Write informative/explanatory texts to examine a topic and convey ideas and information clearly. **Writing 9.b.** Apply grade 5 Reading standards to informational texts (e.g., "Explain how an author uses reasons and evidence to support particular points in a text, identifying which reasons and evidence support which point[s]").

Connect the Texts
Informative/Explanatory Essay

Student Prompt Look back at *Ten Mile Day* and "Working on the Railroad." What factual information does the Web site in the article provide that the story does not? Write a short essay explaining the purpose of each text: to inform, to persuade, or to entertain. Carefully reread both texts to find facts, concrete details, and accurate quotations to support your explanation.

_____

_____

_____

_____

_____

_____

_____

_____

_____

_____

_____

_____

_____

_____

_____

_____

_____

_____

_____

Connect the Texts
Informative/Explanatory Essay

Student Prompt, p. 24 Look back at *Ten Mile Day* and "Working on the Railroad." What factual information does the Web site in the article provide that the story does not? Write a short essay explaining the purpose of each text: to inform, to persuade, or to entertain. Carefully reread both texts to find facts, concrete details, and accurate quotations to support your explanation.

Writing to Sources Discuss with students how *Ten Mile Day* and "Working on the Railroad" present information about the building of the first transcontinental railroad. Then have them carefully reread the story and the article to find the purpose of each text. Students' paragraphs should include accurate quotations, concrete details, and facts from the texts to support their conclusions.

			Informative/Explanatory Writing Rubric		
Score	**Focus**	**Organization**	**Development of Evidence**	**Language and Vocabulary**	**Conventions**
4	Main idea is clearly conveyed and well supported; response is focused.	Organization is clear and effective, creating a sense of cohesion.	Evidence is relevant and thorough; includes facts and details.	Ideas are clearly and effectively conveyed, using precise language and/or domain-specific vocabulary.	Command of conventions is strongly demonstrated.
3	Main idea is clear, adequately supported; response is generally focused.	Organization is clear, though minor flaws may be present and some ideas may be disconnected.	Evidence is adequate and includes facts and details.	Ideas are adequately conveyed, using both precise and more general language; may include domain-specific vocabulary.	Command of conventions is sufficiently demonstrated.
2	Main idea is somewhat supported; lacks focus or includes unnecessary material.	Organization is inconsistent, and flaws are apparent.	Evidence is uneven or incomplete; insufficient use of facts and details.	Ideas are unevenly conveyed, using overly-simplistic language; lacks domain-specific vocabulary.	Command of conventions is uneven.
1	Response may be confusing, unfocused; main idea insufficiently supported.	Organization is poor or nonexistent.	Evidence is poor or nonexistent.	Ideas are conveyed in a vague, unclear, or confusing manner.	There is very little command of conventions.
0	The response shows no evidence of the ability to construct a coherent explanatory essay using information from sources.				

© **Common Core State Standards**

Writing 2. Write informative/explanatory texts to examine a topic and convey ideas and information clearly. **Writing 9.b.** Apply grade 5 Reading standards to informational texts (e.g., "Explain how an author uses reasons and evidence to support particular points in a text, identifying which reasons and evidence support which point[s]").

Prove It!
Informative/Explanatory Essay

Academic Vocabulary

In a **problem-solution essay,** a writer explains one or more problems and their solution(s). Problems and solutions appear in separate paragraphs, and often under separate headings, in the body of the essay.

ELL

Introduce Genre Write *problem-solution* on the board. Explain that this type of essay identifies a problem and presents ways to solve it. Discuss with students the key features of a problem-solution essay that appear on this page. Emphasize that headings can be used to format and organize the body of the essay.

Meeting the Challenge of Staying Alive

Informative/Explanatory Problem-Solution Essay

In this unit, students have read examples of informative/explanatory writing and have had the opportunity to write in this mode. Remind students of texts and writing tasks (such as Write Like a Reporter and Connect the Texts) in which they have encountered and practiced informative/explanatory writing.

Key Features of an Informative/Explanatory Problem-Solution Essay

- provides a general focus on the problem(s) and solution(s) in the introduction
- groups related information logically
- includes formatting when useful in aiding comprehension
- develops the topic with facts, definitions, details, quotations, or other information
- connects ideas by using transitional words, phrases, and clauses
- uses precise language and domain-specific vocabulary
- provides a concluding statement or section related to the topic

Writing Task Overview

Each unit writing task provides students with an opportunity to write to sources. To successfully complete the task, students must analyze, synthesize, and evaluate multiple complex texts and create their own written response.

Meeting the Challenge of Staying Alive

Part 1: Students will read and take notes on the selected sources. They will then respond to several questions about these sources and discuss their written responses with partners or in small groups.

Part 2: Students will work individually to plan, write, and revise their own informative/explanatory problem-solution essay.

Scorable Products: evidence-based short responses, informative/explanatory problem-solution essay

Meeting the Challenge of Staying Alive: Writing Task – Short Response

Teacher Directions:

1. **Introduce the Sources** Refer students to the following texts in the Student Edition:

   1. *Red Kayak,* pp. 26–41

   2. *Island of the Blue Dolphins,* pp. 88–99

   3. "Seven Survival Questions," pp. 104–107

   Explain to students that they will need to draw evidence and support from the texts above in order to answer evidence-based short response questions and to write an informative/explanatory problem-solution essay. Students should take notes and categorize information as they closely reread the texts. Students should be given paper or a relevant graphic organizer from the TR DVD for note-taking.

2. **Provide Student Directions and Scoring Information (p. 30)** Answer any task-related questions students may have. If necessary, provide additional paper for students to write their responses.

3. **Initiate the Writing Task** If you are timing this part of the task, you may wish to alert students when half the allotted time has elapsed and again when 5 minutes remain.

4. **Facilitate Collaboration** After students have completed their written responses to the evidence-based short response questions, assign partners and have them discuss their responses. If students struggle to work together productively, model ways for them to express their ideas, ask for information or further clarification, and build on the remarks of others.

©️ Common Core State Standards

Writing 2. Write informative/explanatory texts to examine a topic and convey ideas and information clearly. **Speaking/Listening 1.** Engage effectively in a range of collaborative discussions (one-on-one, in groups, and teacher-led) with diverse partners on grade 5 topics and texts, building on others' ideas and expressing their own clearly. **(Also Writing 2.a., Writing 2.b., Writing 2.c., Writing 2.d., Writing 2.e.)**

Scoring Information

Use the following 2-point scoring rubrics to evaluate students' answers to the evidence-based short response questions.

1. Using details in the three selections, explain how people and characters respond to the problem of staying alive or helping others to stay alive. How are the problems they face and their solutions to the problems similar and different?

	Analysis Rubric
2	The response: • demonstrates the ability to analyze similarities and differences among the problems and solutions • includes specific details that make reference to the texts
1	The response: • demonstrates a limited ability to analyze similarities and differences among the problems and solutions • includes some details that make reference to the texts
0	A response receives no credit if it demonstrates no ability to analyze similarities and differences among problems and solutions or includes no relevant details from the texts.

2. Combine problems in the three selections to describe one new problem a person might face in nature, such as being stranded in the woods and having to make a shelter for the night. Refer to key words and phrases from the texts.

	Synthesis Rubric
2	The response: • demonstrates the ability to synthesize information from the sources in order to describe a problem • includes specific details that make reference to the texts
1	The response: • demonstrates a limited ability to synthesize information from the sources in order to describe a problem • includes some details that make reference to the texts
0	A response receives no credit if it demonstrates no ability to synthesize information from the sources or includes no relevant details from the texts.

3. Suppose you faced the problem that you identified in the second question. Decide which of the solutions that you read about you would use first. Which would you use second and third? Use details from the three texts to rank solutions in order of importance and explain your reasoning.

	Evaluation Rubric	
2	The response: • demonstrates the ability to evaluate texts in order to propose and rank solutions • includes specific details that make reference to the texts
1	The response: • demonstrates a limited ability to evaluate texts in order to propose and rank solutions • includes some details that make reference to the texts
0	A response receives no credit if it demonstrates no ability to evaluate information from the sources or includes no relevant details from the texts.

© **Common Core State Standards**

Writing 8. Recall relevant information from experiences or gather relevant information from print and digital sources; summarize or paraphrase information in notes and finished work, and provide a list of sources. **Writing 9.** Draw evidence from literary or informational texts to support analysis, reflection, and research. **Writing 9.a.** Apply grade 5 Reading standards to literature (e.g., "Compare and contrast two or more characters, settings, or events in a story or a drama, drawing on specific details in the text [e.g., how characters interact]").

Meeting the Challenge of Staying Alive:
Writing Task – Short Response

Student Directions:

Your Assignment You will reread several selections from Unit 1 and take notes on these sources. Then you will answer three questions about these materials. You may refer to your notes or to any of the sources as often as you like.

Sources

1. *Red Kayak,* pp. 26–41

2. *Island of the Blue Dolphins,* pp. 88–99

3. "Seven Survival Questions," pp. 104–107

Be sure to read closely and take good notes. Your sources and notes will be the basis for writing your own problem-solution essay in the second half of this writing task.

Evidence-Based Short Response Questions Answer the short response questions on the lines provided below each question. Your answers to these questions will be scored. Be sure to base your answers on the sources you have just read. Remember that you may refer back to your notes or to any of the sources.

After you have answered the questions, you will discuss your responses with a partner. Your teacher will let you know when to begin the discussion part of this task.

Scoring Information Your responses will be scored based on evidence of your ability to:

- compare and contrast information from multiple texts
- include details and examples from each source
- identify, analyze, synthesize, and evaluate information from the sources

Evidence-Based Short Response Questions

1. Using details in the three selections, explain how people and characters respond to the problem of staying alive or helping others to stay alive. How are the problems they face and their solutions to the problems similar and different?

_____

_____

_____

_____

2. Combine problems in the three selections to identify one new problem a person might face in nature, such as being stranded in the woods and having to make a shelter for the night. Refer to key words and phrases from the texts.

_____

_____

_____

_____

3. Suppose you faced the problem that you identified in the second question. Decide which of the solutions that you read about you would use first. Which would you use second and third? Use details from the three texts to rank solutions in order of importance and explain your reasoning.

_____

_____

_____

_____

Collaborative Discussion

After you have written your responses to the questions, discuss your ideas. Your teacher will assign you a partner and let you know when to begin.

Meeting the Challenge of Staying Alive: Writing Task – Essay

Teacher Directions:

1. **Provide Student Directions and Scoring Information (p. 34)** Explain to students that they will now review their notes and sources, and plan, draft, and revise their informative/explanatory problem-solution essays. Although they may use their notes and sources, they must work alone. Students will be allowed to look back at the answers they wrote to the short responses, but they are not allowed to make changes to those answers. Have students read the directions for the essay and answer any task-related questions they may have. Students should be given paper on which to write their problem-solution essays.

2. **Initiate the Writing Task** If you are timing this part of the task, you may wish to suggest approximate times for students to begin writing and revising. If students wish to continue writing rather than revising, allow them to do so. Alert students when 5 minutes remain.

3. **Scoring Information** Use the scoring rubric on the next page to evaluate students' problem-solution essays.

4. **Essay Prompt** Use what you have learned from reading *Red Kayak, Island of the Blue Dolphins*, and "Seven Survival Questions." Write a problem-solution essay that explains how to meet the challenge of staying alive. Using details and examples from the three texts, explain the specific problem and present one or more detailed solutions. Use headings to identify your problem and solution(s).

4-point Informative/Explanatory Writing Rubric					
Score	**Focus**	**Organization**	**Development of Evidence**	**Language and Vocabulary**	**Conventions**
4	The problem-solution essay is clearly stated, focused, and strongly maintained.	The problem-solution essay has a clear and logical structure and connects ideas effectively.	The problem-solution essay provides thorough and convincing support that includes facts and details.	The problem-solution essay clearly and effectively expresses ideas, using precise language and appropriate vocabulary.	The problem-solution essay demonstrates a strong command of conventions.
3	The problem-solution essay is mostly focused, though some loosely related material may be present.	The problem-solution essay has a clear structure, though there may be minor flaws and some ideas may be loosely connected.	The problem-solution essay provides adequate support that includes facts and details.	The problem-solution essay adequately expresses ideas, using precise and mostly appropriate vocabulary.	The problem-solution essay demonstrates an adequate command of conventions.
2	The problem-solution essay is somewhat focused with some extraneous material or a minor drift in focus.	The problem-solution essay has an inconsistent structure, and flaws are evident.	The problem-solution essay provides cursory support that includes partial or uneven use of facts and details.	The problem-solution essay expresses ideas unevenly, using simplistic language.	The problem-solution essay demonstrates a partial command of conventions.
1	The problem-solution essay may be confusing, unfocused, or not sufficiently sustained.	The problem-solution essay has little or no discernible structure.	The problem-solution essay provides minimal support that includes few facts and details.	The problem-solution essay's expression of ideas is vague, confusing, or inappropriate.	The problem-solution essay demonstrates a lack of command of conventions.
0	A response gets no credit if it provides no evidence of the ability to compose a coherent problem-solution essay based on information from the sources.				

Ⓒ **Common Core State Standards**

Writing 2. Write informative/explanatory texts to examine a topic and convey ideas and information clearly. **Writing 9.** Draw evidence from literary or informational texts to support analysis, reflection, and research. **(Also Writing 2.a., Writing 2.b., Writing 2.d., Writing 2.e., Writing 10.)**

Meeting the Challenge of Staying Alive:
Writing Task – Essay

Student Directions:

Your Assignment Now you will review your notes and sources, and plan, draft, and revise your informative/explanatory problem-solution essay. While you may use your notes and refer to the sources, you must work on your own. You may also refer to the answers you wrote to earlier questions, but you cannot change those answers.

Essay Prompt Use what you have learned from reading *Red Kayak, Island of the Blue Dolphins*, and "Seven Survival Questions." Write a problem-solution essay that explains how to meet the challenge of staying alive. Using details and examples from the three texts, explain the specific problem and present one or more detailed solutions. Use headings to identify your problem and solution(s).

Scoring Information Your informative/explanatory problem-solution essay will be assigned a score for

1. **Focus–** how well you provide a focus on the problems and solutions and maintain that focus throughout the essay

2. **Organization–** how well your essay groups related information logically and uses transitional words and phrases

3. **Elaboration–** how well you develop your topic with support, such as facts, definitions, details, and quotations

4. **Language and Vocabulary–** how well you give information using precise language and domain-specific vocabulary

5. **Conventions–** how well you follow the rules of grammar, usage, punctuation, capitalization, and spelling

Now begin work on your problem-solution essay. Try to manage your time carefully so that you can

- plan your problem-solution essay
- write your problem-solution essay
- revise and edit for a final draft

Meeting the Challenge of Staying Alive: Writing Task – Essay

Teacher Directions:

1. Publish Explain to students that publishing their writing is the last step in the writing process. If time permits, have students review one another's essays and incorporate any comments their classmates have. Require word-processed final drafts so that students may practice and improve keyboarding skills. Encourage students to use the Internet to share their work with others.

2. Present Students will now have the option to present their problem-solution essays. Suggest students create one or more visuals to include in their presentations, like a storyboard for their problem and another storyboard or storyboards for their solution(s). Use the list below to offer students some tips on listening and speaking.

While Listening to a Classmate...

- Listen with the purpose of summarizing the problem and its solutions.
- Show encouragement through appropriate facial expressions and body language.

While Speaking to Classmates...

- Help focus your presentation by including—and emphasizing—the headings you wrote.
- Make clear connections between your spoken words and your visuals.
- Make sure everyone can see your visuals.

Things to Do Together...

- Prepare ahead of time: practice your presentation or review what it means to be a good listener.
- Show respect and keep the presentation moving by holding questions and comments until the end.
- Stay on topic as you ask and respond to questions and elaborate on what others have said.

© Common Core State Standards

Writing 6. With some guidance and support from adults, use technology, including the Internet, to produce and publish writing as well as to interact and collaborate with others; demonstrate sufficient command of keyboarding skills to type a minimum of two pages in a single sitting. **Speaking/Listening 1.c.** Pose and respond to specific questions by making comments that contribute to the discussion and elaborate on the remarks of others. **Speaking/Listening 5.** Include multimedia components (e.g., graphics, sound) and visual displays in presentations when appropriate to enhance the development of main ideas or themes. **(Also Speaking/Listening 1.)**

Unit 2 Doing the Right Thing

Writing Focus: Narrative

Write Like a Reporter
Narrative Skit

> **Student Prompt** Reread the section on pp. 188–192 and retell the sequence of events that take place on the reef and the direct aftermath. Make notes on the characters, setting, and events. Then write a short skit based on details from the story. Introduce the story's characters to orient readers. Use dialogue to develop experiences and events. Make sure that the sequence of events unfolds naturally.

_____

_____

_____

_____

_____

_____

_____

_____

_____

_____

_____

_____

_____

_____

_____

_____

_____

Write Like a Reporter
Narrative Skit

> **Student Prompt, p. 38** Reread the section on pp. 188–192 and retell the sequence of events that take place on the reef and the direct aftermath. Make notes on the characters, setting, and events. Then write a short skit based on details from the story. Introduce the story's characters to orient readers. Use dialogue to develop experiences and events. Make sure that the sequence of events unfolds naturally.

Writing to Sources After students reread the section, have them list each event that occurs in sequence, as well as details of the action, main characters, and setting. Remind them to write their narratives in the form of a skit. In their narratives, students should develop characters from *At the Beach* and focus on presenting the main events of the story through dialogue. Remind students to reread the text carefully and base their dialogue and descriptions on details from the original story.

Students' skits should:

- orient the reader by introducing characters
- organize an event sequence that unfolds naturally
- use narrative techniques, such as dialogue, to develop experiences and events
- demonstrate strong command of the conventions of standard written English

---

© Common Core State Standards

Writing 3. Write narratives to develop real or imagined experiences or events using effective technique, descriptive details, and clear event sequences. **Writing 9.a.** Apply grade 5 Reading standards to literature (e.g., "Compare and contrast two or more characters, settings, or events in a story or a drama, drawing on specific details in the text [e.g., how characters interact]").

Connect the Texts
Narrative Article

> **Student Prompt** Reread *At the Beach* and the legend "The Eagle and the Bat" and focus on the lessons the characters learn about honorable behavior. Use details from both texts to write a short newspaper article that retells the events from both stories with emphasis on their differing outcomes. Carefully reread both texts and include details from the texts in your article.

_____

_____

_____

_____

_____

_____

_____

_____

_____

_____

_____

_____

_____

_____

_____

Connect the Texts
Narrative Article

Student Prompt, p. 40 Reread *At the Beach* and the legend "The Eagle and the Bat" and focus on the lessons the characters learn about honorable behavior. Use details from both texts to write a short newspaper article that retells the events from both stories with emphasis on their differing outcomes. Carefully reread both texts and include details from the texts in your article.

Writing to Sources Before students reread, discuss with them the lessons the characters learn about honorable behavior. Guide them to think about the difference between confessing to a lie (Fernando) and deliberate trickery (the bat). Then ask students to reread both passages and look for descriptive details they can use to retell the events from both stories. Students' responses should include details from both texts.

4-point Narrative Writing Rubric					
Score	**Narrative Focus**	**Organization**	**Development of Narrative**	**Language and Vocabulary**	**Conventions**
4	Narrative is clearly focused and developed throughout.	Narrative has a well-developed, logical, easy-to-follow plot.	Narrative includes thorough and effective use of details, dialogue, and description.	Narrative uses precise, concrete sensory language as well as figurative language and/or domain-specific vocabulary.	Narrative has correct grammar, usage, spelling, capitalization, and punctuation.
3	Narrative is mostly focused and developed throughout.	Narrative has a plot, but there may be some lack of clarity and/or unrelated events.	Narrative includes adequate use of details, dialogue and description.	Narrative uses adequate sensory and figurative language and/or domain-specific vocabulary.	Narrative has a few errors but is completely understandable.
2	Narrative is somewhat developed but may occasionally lose focus.	Narrative's plot is difficult to follow, and ideas are not connected well.	Narrative includes only a few details, dialogues, and descriptions.	Language in narrative is not precise or sensory; lacks domain-specific vocabulary.	Narrative has some errors in usage, grammar, spelling and/or punctuation.
1	Narrative may be confusing, unfocused, or too short.	Narrative has little or no apparent plot.	Narrative includes few or no details, dialogue or description.	Language in narrative is vague, unclear, or confusing.	Narrative is hard to follow because of frequent errors.
0	Narrative gets no credit if it does not demonstrate adequate command of narrative writing traits.				

© Common Core State Standards

Writing 3. Write narratives to develop real or imagined experiences or events using effective technique, descriptive details, and clear event sequences. **Writing 9.a.** Apply grade 5 Reading standards to literature (e.g., "Compare and contrast two or more characters, settings, or events in a story or a drama, drawing on specific details in the text [e.g., how characters interact]").

Write Like a Reporter
Narrative Paragraph

> **Student Prompt** Reread the section on pp. 213–216 and retell the sequence of events on the day of the battle. Use details from the text to write a one-paragraph fantasy retelling the experiences from the flag's perspective. Establish the situation in the story and organize the events in a natural way. Make sure to include pacing similar to that of the original text in your narrative.

_____

_____

_____

_____

_____

_____

_____

_____

_____

_____

_____

_____

_____

_____

_____

_____

Write Like a Reporter
Narrative Paragraph

Student Prompt, p. 42 Reread the section on pp. 213–216 and retell the sequence of events on the day of the battle. Use details from the text to write a one-paragraph fantasy retelling the experiences from the flag's perspective. Establish the situation in the story and organize the events in a natural way. Make sure to include pacing similar to that of the original text in your narrative.

Writing to Sources After students reread this section from *Hold the Flag High*, have them identify relevant details about the battle, including characters and the setting. Before students begin writing, remind them that their fantasy narratives should clearly establish the situation and present events in a natural way. The paragraphs should also use the narrative technique of pacing to convey information about the situations featured in the story.

Students' paragraphs should:

- orient the reader by establishing a situation
- organize an event sequence that unfolds naturally
- use narrative techniques, such as pacing, to develop experiences and events
- demonstrate strong command of the conventions of standard written English

© **Common Core State Standards**

Writing 3. Write narratives to develop real or imagined experiences or events using effective technique, descriptive details, and clear event sequences. **Writing 9.b.** Apply grade 5 Reading standards to informational texts (e.g., "Explain how an author uses reasons and evidence to support particular points in a text, identifying which reasons and evidence support which point[s]").

Name _____

Connect the Texts
Narrative Story

> **Student Prompt** Reread *Hold the Flag High* and "How to Fold the American Flag" and pay attention to the facts and details both texts give about how to treat the American flag. Then write a narrative story about a fictional character who carries the flag and folds it up after he or she is finished. Carefully reread both texts and include details from both texts in your narrative as you describe the events and processes. Include transitions that help make the sequence clear.

_____

_____

_____

_____

_____

_____

_____

_____

_____

_____

_____

_____

_____

_____

_____

_____

_____

_____

Connect the Texts
Narrative Story

Student Prompt, p. 44 Reread *Hold the Flag High* and "How to Fold the American Flag" and pay attention to the facts and details both texts give about how to treat the American flag. Then write a narrative story about a fictional character who carries the flag and folds it up after he or she is finished. Carefully reread both texts and include details from both texts in your narrative as you describe the events and processes. Include transitions that help make the sequence clear.

Writing to Sources Before students reread, discuss with them the importance of respecting the American flag as both a national symbol and as a symbol of freedom. Then ask students to reread both texts and look for details and facts about how someone shows respect for the flag. Students' narrative stories should include details from both texts, as well as a clear sequence of events.

4-point Narrative Writing Rubric					
Score	**Narrative Focus**	**Organization**	**Development of Narrative**	**Language and Vocabulary**	**Conventions**
4	Narrative is clearly focused and developed throughout.	Narrative has a well-developed, logical, easy-to-follow plot.	Narrative includes thorough and effective use of details, dialogue, and description.	Narrative uses precise, concrete sensory language as well as figurative language and/or domain-specific vocabulary.	Narrative has correct grammar, usage, spelling, capitalization, and punctuation.
3	Narrative is mostly focused and developed throughout.	Narrative has a plot, but there may be some lack of clarity and/or unrelated events.	Narrative includes adequate use of details, dialogue and description.	Narrative uses adequate sensory and figurative language and/or domain-specific vocabulary.	Narrative has a few errors but is completely understandable.
2	Narrative is somewhat developed but may occasionally lose focus.	Narrative's plot is difficult to follow, and ideas are not connected well.	Narrative includes only a few details, dialogues, and descriptions.	Language in narrative is not precise or sensory; lacks domain-specific vocabulary.	Narrative has some errors in usage, grammar, spelling and/or punctuation.
1	Narrative may be confusing, unfocused, or too short.	Narrative has little or no apparent plot.	Narrative includes few or no details, dialogue or description.	Language in narrative is vague, unclear, or confusing.	Narrative is hard to follow because of frequent errors.
0	Narrative gets no credit if it does not demonstrate adequate command of narrative writing traits.				

Ⓒ Common Core State Standards

Writing 3. Write narratives to develop real or imagined experiences or events using effective technique, descriptive details, and clear event sequences. **Writing 9.b.** Apply grade 5 Reading standards to informational texts (e.g., "Explain how an author uses reasons and evidence to support particular points in a text, identifying which reasons and evidence support which point[s]").

Write Like a Reporter
Narrative Paragraph

Student Prompt Reread the story on pp. 238–249 and retell the sequence of events. Make notes about the details, characters, and main events. Then write a one-paragraph letter retelling the events from Mrs. Lu's perspective, based on details from the story. Use first-person point of view to establish Mrs. Lu as the narrator. Use transitions, such as *first*, *next*, and *then*, to show the sequence of events. Also include concrete words and phrases to convey experiences and events.

_____

_____

_____

_____

_____

_____

_____

_____

_____

_____

_____

_____

_____

_____

_____

_____

Write Like a Reporter
Narrative Paragraph

> **Student Prompt, p. 46** Reread the story on pp. 238–249 and retell the sequence of events. Make notes about the details, characters, and main events. Then write a one-paragraph letter retelling the events from Mrs. Lu's perspective, based on details from the story. Use first-person point of view to establish Mrs. Lu as the narrator. Use transitions, such as *first, next,* and *then,* to show the sequence of events. Also include concrete words and phrases to convey experiences and events.

Writing to Sources After students reread the *The Chí-lin Purse*, have them take notes on each event that occurs in sequence, as well as details of the plot, the main characters, and the setting. Remind them to write their narrative letters from Mrs. Lu's perspective. In their letters, students should develop the characters and focus on presenting the main events in sequence, using transitions to make the order clear. They should also include concrete words and phrases to convey experiences and events. Remind students to reread the text carefully and base their narrative letters on details from the original story.

Students' paragraphs should:

- orient the reader by organizing events
- use a variety of transitional words
- use concrete words and phrases to convey experiences and events
- demonstrate strong command of the conventions of standard written English

---

Ⓒ **Common Core State Standards**

Writing 3. Write narratives to develop real or imagined experiences or events using effective technique, descriptive details, and clear event sequences. **Writing 9.a.** Apply grade 5 Reading standards to literature (e.g., "Compare and contrast two or more characters, settings, or events in a story or a drama, drawing on specific details in the text [e.g., how characters interact]").

Name _____

Connect the Texts
Narrative Dialogue

Student Prompt Look back at *The Chí-lin Purse* and "The Story of Phan Ku" and consider what Hsiang-ling would say to Phan Ku if they met. Compare and contrast each character's story. Then write a one- or two-paragraph dialogue between Hsiang-ling and Phan Ku that demonstrates how each character makes sacrifices. Include details from both texts to create your narrative. Carefully reread both stories to find specific facts and sensory descriptions to include in your narrative.

_____

_____

_____

_____

_____

_____

_____

_____

_____

_____

_____

_____

Connect the Texts
Narrative Dialogue

Student Prompt, p. 48 Look back at *The Chí-lin Purse* and "The Story of Phan Ku" and consider what Hsiang-ling would say to Phan Ku if they met. Compare and contrast each character's story. Then write a one- or two-paragraph dialogue between Hsiang-ling and Phan Ku that demonstrates how each character makes sacrifices. Include details from both texts to create your narrative. Carefully reread both stories to find specific facts and sensory descriptions to include in your narrative.

Writing to Sources Discuss with students the importance of helping people. Then have students carefully reread *The Chí-lin Purse* and "The Story of Phan Ku" and write a dialogue between Hsiang-ling and Phan Ku that demonstrates their similarities and differences. Remind students to use descriptive details and sensory language from both texts to develop their narratives.

| \multicolumn{6}{c}{**4-point Narrative Writing Rubric**} |
Score	Narrative Focus	Organization	Development of Narrative	Language and Vocabulary	Conventions
4	Narrative is clearly focused and developed throughout.	Narrative has a well-developed, logical, easy-to-follow plot.	Narrative includes thorough and effective use of details, dialogue, and description.	Narrative uses precise, concrete sensory language as well as figurative language and/or domain-specific vocabulary.	Narrative has correct grammar, usage, spelling, capitalization, and punctuation.
3	Narrative is mostly focused and developed throughout.	Narrative has a plot, but there may be some lack of clarity and/or unrelated events.	Narrative includes adequate use of details, dialogue and description.	Narrative uses adequate sensory and figurative language and/or domain-specific vocabulary.	Narrative has a few errors but is completely understandable.
2	Narrative is somewhat developed but may occasionally lose focus.	Narrative's plot is difficult to follow, and ideas are not connected well.	Narrative includes only a few details, dialogues, and descriptions.	Language in narrative is not precise or sensory; lacks domain-specific vocabulary.	Narrative has some errors in usage, grammar, spelling and/or punctuation.
1	Narrative may be confusing, unfocused, or too short.	Narrative has little or no apparent plot.	Narrative includes few or no details, dialogue or description.	Language in narrative is vague, unclear, or confusing.	Narrative is hard to follow because of frequent errors.
0	\multicolumn{5}{l}{Narrative gets no credit if it does not demonstrate adequate command of narrative writing traits.}

© Common Core State Standards

Writing 3. Write narratives to develop real or imagined experiences or events using effective technique, descriptive details, and clear event sequences. **Writing 9.a.** Apply grade 5 Reading standards to literature (e.g., "Compare and contrast two or more characters, settings, or events in a story or a drama, drawing on specific details in the text [e.g., how characters interact]").

Write Like a Reporter
Narrative Paragraph

Student Prompt Reread the story on pp. 266–277 and retell the sequence of events. Use details from the text to write a one-paragraph journal entry retelling the experiences from Tony's perspective, using first-person point of view. Introduce the narrator from the story and organize the events logically. In the journal entry, make sure to include descriptions that show the characters' responses to situations in the story.

_____

_____

_____

_____

_____

_____

_____

_____

_____

_____

_____

_____

_____

_____

_____

_____

_____

_____

Write Like a Reporter
Narrative Paragraph

Student Prompt, p. 50 Reread the story on pp. 266–277 and retell the sequence of events. Use details from the text to write a one-paragraph journal entry retelling the experiences from Tony's perspective, using first-person point of view. Introduce the narrator from the story and organize the events logically. In the journal entry, make sure to include descriptions that show the characters' responses to situations in the story.

Writing to Sources After students reread *A Summer's Trade*, have them identify relevant details about Tony's personality and important events in the story. Before students begin writing, tell them to write their journal entries from a first-person point of view, using *I* instead of *he*. Remind students that their narratives should clearly introduce the narrator and present events in a natural way. The journal entries should also use the narrative technique of description to show the responses of characters to situations.

Students' paragraphs should:

- orient the reader by introducing a narrator
- organize an event sequence that unfolds naturally
- use narrative techniques, such as description, to show the responses of characters to situations
- demonstrate strong command of the conventions of standard written English

© Common Core State Standards

Writing 3. Write narratives to develop real or imagined experiences or events using effective technique, descriptive details, and clear event sequences. **Writing 9.a.** Apply grade 5 Reading standards to literature (e.g., "Compare and contrast two or more characters, settings, or events in a story or a drama, drawing on specific details in the text [e.g., how characters interact]").

Connect the Texts
Narrative Dialogue

Student Prompt Look back at *A Summer's Trade* and "Thunderbird and Killer Whale" and consider what Tony and Killer Whale might say about sacrifices. Compare and contrast each character's story. Then write a short dialogue between Tony and Killer Whale that reveals how each character saved something important. Include details from both texts to create your dialogue. Carefully reread both texts to find specific facts and sensory details to include in your dialogue.

_____

_____

_____

_____

_____

_____

_____

_____

_____

_____

_____

_____

_____

_____

_____

_____

Connect the Texts
Narrative Dialogue

Student Prompt, p. 52 Look back at *A Summer's Trade* and "Thunderbird and Killer Whale" and consider what Tony and Killer Whale might say about sacrifices. Compare and contrast each character's story. Then write a short dialogue between Tony and Killer Whale that reveals how each character saved something important. Include details from both texts to create your dialogue. Carefully reread both texts to find specific facts and sensory details to include in your dialogue.

Writing to Sources Discuss with students the importance of making sacrifices. Then have students carefully reread *A Summer's Trade* and "Thunderbird and Killer Whale." Ask them to write a dialogue between Tony and Killer Whale that demonstrates the stories' similarities and differences. Remind students to use sensory details and descriptive language from both texts to develop their dialogues.

4-point Narrative Writing Rubric				
Score	Narrative Focus	Organization	Development of Narrative	Language and Vocabulary	Conventions
4	Narrative is clearly focused and developed throughout.	Narrative has a well-developed, logical, easy-to-follow plot.	Narrative includes thorough and effective use of details, dialogue, and description.	Narrative uses precise, concrete sensory language as well as figurative language and/or domain-specific vocabulary.	Narrative has correct grammar, usage, spelling, capitalization, and punctuation.
3	Narrative is mostly focused and developed throughout.	Narrative has a plot, but there may be some lack of clarity and/or unrelated events.	Narrative includes adequate use of details, dialogue and description.	Narrative uses adequate sensory and figurative language and/or domain-specific vocabulary.	Narrative has a few errors but is completely understandable.
2	Narrative is somewhat developed but may occasionally lose focus.	Narrative's plot is difficult to follow, and ideas are not connected well.	Narrative includes only a few details, dialogues, and descriptions.	Language in narrative is not precise or sensory; lacks domain-specific vocabulary.	Narrative has some errors in usage, grammar, spelling and/or punctuation.
1	Narrative may be confusing, unfocused, or too short.	Narrative has little or no apparent plot.	Narrative includes few or no details, dialogue or description.	Language in narrative is vague, unclear, or confusing.	Narrative is hard to follow because of frequent errors.
0	Narrative gets no credit if it does not demonstrate adequate command of narrative writing traits.				

© Common Core State Standards

Writing 3. Write narratives to develop real or imagined experiences or events using effective technique, descriptive details, and clear event sequences. **Writing 9.a.** Apply grade 5 Reading standards to literature (e.g., "Compare and contrast two or more characters, settings, or events in a story or a drama, drawing on specific details in the text [e.g., how characters interact]").

Name _____

Write Like a Reporter
Narrative Paragraph

Student Prompt Reread the poem on pp. 296–307 and retell the sequence of events. List the main events as they occur and make notes about the details, characters, and action. Then write a narrative paragraph retelling the events from the point of view of a British soldier, based on details from the poem. Use transitions, such as *after a few hours, later,* and *finally,* to show sequence. Be sure to include sensory details to convey experiences and events.

_____

_____

_____

_____

_____

_____

_____

_____

_____

_____

_____

_____

_____

_____

_____

Write Like a Reporter
Narrative Paragraph

Student Prompt, p. 54 Reread the poem on pp. 296–307 and retell the sequence of events. List the main events as they occur and make notes about the details, characters, and action. Then write a narrative paragraph retelling the events from the point of view of a British soldier, based on details from the poem. Use transitions, such as *after a few hours, later,* and *finally,* to show sequence. Be sure to include sensory details to convey experiences and events.

Writing to Sources After students reread *The Midnight Ride of Paul Revere*, have them focus on chronology, as well as descriptions of the plot, main characters, and setting. Remind them to write their narratives from the perspective of a British soldier. In their narratives, students should develop characters and elaborate on the main events of the story, using a variety of transitional words and phrases to clarify the order of events. They should also include concrete words and phrases to convey experiences and events. Remind students to reread the text carefully and base their narratives on details from the original story.

Students' paragraphs should:

- orient the reader by organizing events
- use a variety of transitional words and phrases
- use sensory details to convey experiences and events
- demonstrate strong command of the conventions of standard written English

© **Common Core State Standards**

Writing 3. Write narratives to develop real or imagined experiences or events using effective technique, descriptive details, and clear event sequences. **Writing 9.a.** Apply grade 5 Reading standards to literature (e.g., "Compare and contrast two or more characters, settings, or events in a story or a drama, drawing on specific details in the text [e.g., how characters interact]").

Connect the Texts
Narrative Letter

Student Prompt Look back at *The Midnight Ride of Paul Revere* and "The Heroic Paul Revere." Compare and contrast both versions of the story and the way both texts organize and present similar information. Then write a one-paragraph letter from Paul Revere's perspective. Include details from both texts to create your narrative. Carefully reread the selections to find specific facts and sensory descriptions to include in your narrative.

_____

_____

_____

_____

_____

_____

_____

_____

_____

_____

_____

_____

_____

_____

_____

_____

Connect the Texts
Narrative Letter

> **Student Prompt, p. 56** Look back at *The Midnight Ride of Paul Revere* and "The Heroic Paul Revere." Compare and contrast both versions of the story and the way both texts organize and present similar information. Then write a one-paragraph letter from Paul Revere's perspective. Include details from both texts to create your narrative. Carefully reread the selections to find specific facts and sensory descriptions to include in your narrative.

Writing to Sources Before students reread, remind them that "The Heroic Paul Revere" is an adaptation of *The Midnight Ride of Paul Revere*. Discuss with students how the same information can be presented and organized in different ways. Then have students carefully reread both texts and write a narrative letter by Paul Revere that demonstrates another way to organize this information. Remind students to use descriptive language and sensory details from both texts to develop their narratives.

	4-point Narrative Writing Rubric				
Score	**Narrative Focus**	**Organization**	**Development of Narrative**	**Language and Vocabulary**	**Conventions**
4	Narrative is clearly focused and developed throughout.	Narrative has a well-developed, logical, easy-to-follow plot.	Narrative includes thorough and effective use of details, dialogue, and description.	Narrative uses precise, concrete sensory language as well as figurative language and/or domain-specific vocabulary.	Narrative has correct grammar, usage, spelling, capitalization, and punctuation.
3	Narrative is mostly focused and developed throughout.	Narrative has a plot, but there may be some lack of clarity and/or unrelated events.	Narrative includes adequate use of details, dialogue and description.	Narrative uses adequate sensory and figurative language and/or domain-specific vocabulary.	Narrative has a few errors but is completely understandable.
2	Narrative is somewhat developed but may occasionally lose focus.	Narrative's plot is difficult to follow, and ideas are not connected well.	Narrative includes only a few details, dialogues, and descriptions.	Language in narrative is not precise or sensory; lacks domain-specific vocabulary.	Narrative has some errors in usage, grammar, spelling and/or punctuation.
1	Narrative may be confusing, unfocused, or too short.	Narrative has little or no apparent plot.	Narrative includes few or no details, dialogue or description.	Language in narrative is vague, unclear, or confusing.	Narrative is hard to follow because of frequent errors.
0	Narrative gets no credit if it does not demonstrate adequate command of narrative writing traits.				

Ⓒ Common Core State Standards

Writing 3. Write narratives to develop real or imagined experiences or events using effective technique, descriptive details, and clear event sequences. **Writing 9.a.** Apply grade 5 Reading standards to literature (e.g., "Compare and contrast two or more characters, settings, or events in a story or a drama, drawing on specific details in the text [e.g., how characters interact]").

Prove It!
Narrative Short Story

Plotting a Surprise

Narrative Short Story

In this unit, students have read examples of narrative writing, including a short story, and have had the opportunity to write in this mode. Remind students of texts and writing tasks (such as Write Like a Reporter and Connect the Texts) in which they have encountered and practiced narrative writing.

Key Features of a Short Story

- introduces and develops a situation, a narrator, and characters
- organizes events in logical order
- includes an effective opening, dialogue, pacing, and description
- uses transition words, phrases, and clauses to show sequence
- uses precise words and phrases, descriptive details, and sensory language
- includes a satisfying conclusion

Writing Task Overview

Each unit writing task provides students with an opportunity to write to sources. To successfully complete the task, students must analyze, synthesize, and evaluate multiple complex texts and create their own written response.

Plotting a Surprise

Part 1: Students will reread and take notes on the selected sources. They will then respond to several questions about these sources and discuss their written responses with partners or in small groups.

Part 2: Students will work individually to plan, write, and revise their own short story.

Scorable Products: short responses, short story

Plotting a Surprise: Writing Task – Short Response

Teacher Directions:

1. **Introduce the Sources** Refer students to the following texts in the Student Edition:

   1. *At the Beach,* pp. 182–193

   2. *The Chí-lin Purse,* pp. 236–249

   3. *A Summer's Trade,* pp. 264–277

   Explain to students that they will need to draw evidence and support from the texts above in order to answer evidence-based short response questions and to write a short story. Students should take notes on narrative structures and strategies as they closely reread the texts. Students should be given paper or a relevant graphic organizer from the TR DVD for note-taking.

2. **Provide Student Directions and Scoring Information (p. 62)** Answer any task-related questions students may have. If necessary, provide additional paper for students to write their responses.

3. **Initiate the Writing Task** If you are timing this part of the task, you may wish to alert students when half the allotted time has elapsed and again when 5 minutes remain.

4. **Facilitate Collaboration** After students have completed their written responses to the evidence-based short response questions, assign partners and have them discuss their responses. Have students take turns reading their responses aloud, asking questions, and responding to those questions with details and text evidence. Partners should alternate roles for each question.

Ⓒ **Common Core State Standards**

Writing 3. Write narratives to develop real or imagined experiences or events using effective technique, descriptive details, and clear event sequences. **Speaking/Listening 1.** Engage effectively in a range of collaborative discussions (one-on-one, in groups, and teacher-led) with diverse partners on grade 5 topics and texts, building on others' ideas and expressing their own clearly. (**Also Writing 3.a., Writing 3.b., Writing 3.c., Writing 3.d., Writing 3.e.**)

Scoring Information

Use the following 2-point scoring rubrics to evaluate students' answers to the evidence-based short response questions.

1. How does each story begin? What is the first event in each plot? Compare the ways the authors of the stories introduce the characters and orient the reader to the situation. Use details from each source to support your answer.

	Analysis Rubric
2	The response: • demonstrates the ability to analyze similarities and differences between the beginnings of stories • includes specific details that make reference to the texts
1	The response: • demonstrates a limited ability to analyze similarities and differences between the beginnings of stories • includes some details that make reference to the texts
0	A response receives no credit if it demonstrates no ability to analyze similarities and differences between the beginnings of stories or includes no relevant details from the texts.

2. Each story ends happily for the main character. In what other way or ways are the endings of all the stories alike? Create a list of similarities, citing specific details from each story.

	Synthesis Rubric
2	The response: • demonstrates the ability to synthesize information from the sources in order to draw an overall conclusion • includes specific details that make reference to the texts
1	The response: • demonstrates a limited ability to synthesize information from the sources in order to draw an overall conclusion • includes some details that make reference to the texts
0	A response receives no credit if it demonstrates no ability to synthesize information from the sources or includes no relevant details from the texts.

3. Determine which story has the best plot and most satisfying ending. Refer to details from each text to support your evaluation, using these details to explain why you think the plot and ending of one story are better than those of the other stories.

Evaluation Rubric	
2	The response: • demonstrates the ability to evaluate the effectiveness of story plots and endings • includes specific details that make reference to the texts
1	The response: • demonstrates a limited ability to evaluate the effectiveness of story plots and endings • includes some details that make reference to the texts
0	A response receives no credit if it demonstrates no ability to evaluate plots and endings or includes no relevant details from the texts.

ⓒ **Common Core State Standards**

Writing 8. Recall relevant information from experiences or gather relevant information from print and digital sources; summarize or paraphrase information in notes and finished work, and provide a list of sources. **Writing 9.** Draw evidence from literary or informational texts to support analysis, reflection, and research.

Plotting a Surprise
Writing Task – Short Response

Student Directions:

Your Assignment You will reread several selections from Unit 2 and take notes on these sources. Then you will answer three questions about these materials. You may refer to your notes or to any of the sources as often as you like.

Sources

1. *At the Beach,* pp. 182–193

2. *The Chí-lin Purse,* pp. 236–249

3. *A Summer's Trade,* pp. 264–277

Be sure to read closely and take good notes. Your sources and notes will be the basis for writing your own short story in the second half of this writing task.

Evidence-Based Short Response Questions Answer the short response questions on the lines provided below each question. Your answers to these questions will be scored. Be sure to base your answers on the sources you have just read. Remember that you may refer back to your notes or to any of the sources.

After you have answered the questions, you will discuss your responses with a partner. Your teacher will let you know when to begin the discussion part of this task.

Scoring Information Your responses will be scored based on how you demonstrate the ability to:

- compare information across texts
- include specific details and examples from the sources
- identify, analyze, synthesize, and evaluate information from the sources
- distinguish key details and support from unnecessary information

Evidence-Based Short Response Questions

1. How does each story begin? What is the first event in each plot? Compare the ways the authors of the stories introduce the characters and orient the reader to the situation. Use details from each source to support your answer.

_____

_____

_____

_____

2. Each story ends happily for the main character. In what other way or ways are the endings of all the stories alike? Create a list of similarities, citing specific details from each story.

_____

_____

_____

_____

3. Determine which story has the best plot and most satisfying ending. Refer to details from each text to support your evaluation, using these details to explain why you think the plot and ending of one story are better than those of the other stories.

_____

_____

_____

_____

Collaborative Discussion

After you have written your responses to the questions, discuss your ideas. Your teacher will assign you a partner and let you know when to begin.

Plotting a Surprise: Writing Task – Short Story

Teacher Directions:

1. **Provide Student Directions and Scoring Information (p. 66)** Explain to students that they will now review their notes and sources, and plan, draft, and revise their short stories. Although they may use their notes and sources, they must work alone. Students will be allowed to look back at the answers they wrote to the short response questions, but they will not be allowed to make changes to those answers. Have students read the directions for the short story and answer any task-related questions they may have. Students should be given paper on which to write their short stories.

2. **Initiate the Writing Task** If you are timing this part of the task, you may wish to suggest approximate times for students to begin writing and revising. If students wish to continue writing rather than revising, allow them to do so. Alert students when 5 minutes remain.

3. **Scoring Information** Use the scoring rubric on the next page to evaluate students' short stories.

4. **Short Story Prompt** Use what you have learned from reading *At the Beach, The Chí-lin Purse,* and *A Summer's Trade* to write a realistic short story with a plot that includes a clear sequence of events leading to a surprise ending. Refer to the three stories you reread to help you develop and organize the plot and provide a satisfying and surprising conclusion. Be sure to follow the conventions of written English.

4-Point Narrative Writing Rubric

Score	Narrative Focus	Organization	Development of Narrative	Language and Vocabulary	Conventions
4	Short story is clearly focused and developed throughout.	Short story has a well-developed, logical, easy-to-follow plot.	Short story includes thorough and effective use of details, pacing, dialogue, and description.	Short story uses precise, concrete sensory language as well as figurative language.	Short story has correct grammar, usage, spelling, capitalization, and punctuation.
3	Short story is mostly focused and developed throughout.	Short story has a plot, but there may be some lack of clarity and/or unrelated events.	Short story includes adequate use of details, pacing, dialogue, and description.	Short story uses adequate sensory and figurative language.	Short story has a few errors but is completely understandable.
2	Short story is somewhat developed but may occasionally lose focus.	Short story's plot is difficult to follow, and ideas are not connected well.	Short story includes only a few details, dialogues, and descriptions.	Language in short story is not concrete, precise, or sensory.	Short story has some errors in usage, grammar, spelling, and/or punctuation.
1	Short story may be confusing, unfocused, or too short.	Short story has little or no apparent plot.	Short story includes few or no details, dialogue, or description.	Language in short story is vague, unclear, or confusing.	Short story is hard to follow because of frequent errors.
0	Short story gets no credit if it does not demonstrate adequate command of narrative writing traits.				

© Common Core State Standards

Writing 3. Write narratives to develop real or imagined experiences or events using effective technique, descriptive details, and clear event sequences. **Writing 9.** Draw evidence from literary or informational texts to support analysis, reflection, and research. (**Also Writing 3.a.,** **Writing 3.b., Writing 10.**)

Plotting a Surprise
Writing Task – Short Story

Student Directions:

Your Assignment Now you will review your notes and sources, and plan, draft, and revise your short story. While you may use your notes and refer to the sources, you must work on your own. You may also refer to the answers you wrote to earlier questions, but you cannot change those answers.

Short Story Prompt Use what you have learned from reading *At the Beach, The Chí-lin Purse,* and *A Summer's Trade* to write a realistic short story with a plot that includes a clear sequence of events leading to a surprise ending. Refer to the three stories you reread to help you develop and organize the plot and provide a satisfying and surprising conclusion. Be sure to follow the conventions of written English.

Scoring Information Your short story will be assigned a score for

1. **Focus –** how well you create a realistic situation and introduce the narrator and characters

2. **Organization –** how well you organize a clear order of events, using transitions to show sequence

3. **Elaboration –** how well you use dialogue, pacing, and description to reveal and develop events and characters

4. **Language and Vocabulary –** how well you use precise words, details, and sensory language

5. **Conventions –** how well you follow the rules of grammar, usage, capitalization, punctuation, and spelling

Now begin work on your short story. Try to manage your time carefully so that you can:

- plan your short story
- write your short story
- revise and edit for a final draft

Plotting a Surprise: Writing Task – Short Story

Teacher Directions:

1. Publish Explain to students that publishing their writing is the last step in the writing process. If time permits, have students review one another's short stories and incorporate any comments their classmates have. Offer students suggestions for how to publish their work online, such as in an e-zine, on a family web page, or as a blog post.

2. Present Students will now have the option to present their short stories. Ask each student to read his or her story to the class and then lead a question-and-answer session about it. Use the list below to offer students some tips on listening and speaking.

While Listening to a Classmate...

- Be prepared to summarize the story's main events.
- Visualize how characters look and what they do.

While Speaking to Classmates...

- Vary your voice as you read dialogue to show differences among characters.
- Stand up straight, but not stiff, and make eye contact.
- Adjust your pace and volume to build suspense and keep your audience interested.

Things to Do Together...

- Know what you want to say before you start to speak and get right to the point.
- Ask and answer questions with detail.
- Build on each other's ideas.

© Common Core State Standards

Writing 6. With some guidance and support from adults, use technology, including the Internet, to produce and publish writing as well as to interact and collaborate with others; demonstrate sufficient command of keyboarding skills to type a minimum of two pages in a single sitting. **Speaking/Listening 1.c.** Pose and respond to specific questions by making comments that contribute to the discussion and elaborate on the remarks of others. **Speaking/Listening 2.** Summarize a written text read aloud or information presented in diverse media and formats, including visually, quantitatively, and orally. **Speaking/Listening 4.** Report on a topic or text or present an opinion, sequencing ideas logically and using appropriate facts and relevant, descriptive details to support main ideas or themes; speak clearly at an understandable pace.

Unit 3 Inventors and Artists

Writing Focus: Argument

Write Like a Reporter

Argumentative Paragraph

Student Prompt Reread *The Fabulous Perpetual Motion Machine* and take careful notes about the construction and outcome of the project. Do you agree or disagree that the perpetual motion machine should be called "fabulous"? Write a paragraph that states your opinion, and support your claim with relevant evidence and details from the text. Use linking phrases, such as *for instance, in order to,* and *in addition,* to make your reasoning clear.

_____

_____

_____

_____

_____

_____

_____

_____

_____

_____

_____

_____

_____

_____

_____

_____

Write Like a Reporter
Argumentative Paragraph

> **Student Prompt, p. 70** Reread *The Fabulous Perpetual Motion Machine* and take careful notes about the construction and outcome of the project. Do you agree or disagree that the perpetual motion machine should be called "fabulous"? Write a paragraph that states your opinion, and support your claim with relevant evidence and details from the text. Use linking phrases, such as *for instance, in order to,* and *in addition,* to make your reasoning clear.

Writing to Sources Before students reread, remind them of one dictionary definition of the word *fabulous* (e.g., "of or related to a fable; mystical, legendary"). Ask students to reread the drama with this definition in mind. Then have them write a paragraph that states whether they agree or disagree that "fabulous" effectively describes the machine. Remind them to base their opinion on details from the text. Also remind them to include linking words to clarify their reasoning.

Students' paragraphs should:

- clearly state an opinion regarding the use of the adjective to describe the machine
- support the opinion with relevant evidence
- link opinion and reasons using phrases
- demonstrate strong command of the conventions of standard written English

---

© Common Core State Standards

Writing 1. Write opinion pieces on topics or texts, supporting a point of view with reasons and information. **Writing 9.a.** Apply grade 5 Reading standards to literature (e.g., "Compare and contrast two or more characters, settings, or events in a story or a drama, drawing on specific details in the text [e.g., how characters interact]").

Connect the Texts
Argumentative Essay

Student Prompt Look back at *The Fabulous Perpetual Motion Machine* and "The Toy Space Shuttle Is Here!" Compare and contrast the information on the two gadgets. Which invention is more likely to work successfully? State your opinion in a short essay that uses facts, concrete details, and accurate quotations from both texts. Conclude with a sentence that clarifies your reasoning.

_____

_____

_____

_____

_____

_____

_____

_____

_____

_____

_____

_____

_____

_____

_____

_____

_____

_____

Connect the Texts
Argumentative Essay

Student Prompt, p. 72 Look back at *The Fabulous Perpetual Motion Machine* and "The Toy Space Shuttle Is Here!" Compare and contrast the information on the two gadgets. Which invention is more likely to work successfully? State your opinion in a short essay that uses facts, concrete details, and accurate quotations from both texts. Conclude with a sentence that clarifies your reasoning.

Writing to Sources After students reread both texts, ask them to point out the main facts of the perpetual motion machine and the toy space shuttle. Discuss with students their opinions on which invention is most likely to be a success. Then have them support their opinions in a short essay that draws evidence from both texts. Remind them to include a concluding sentence that summarizes their opinions and clarifies their reasoning.

Score	Statement of Purpose/Focus	Organization	Development of Evidence	Language and Vocabulary	Conventions
4-point Argument Writing Rubric					
4	Opinion is clearly conveyed and well supported; response is focused.	Organization is clear and effective, creating a sense of cohesion.	Evidence is thorough and persuasive, and includes facts and details.	Ideas are clearly and effectively conveyed, using precise language and/or domain-specific vocabulary.	Command of conventions is strongly demonstrated.
3	Opinion is clear, adequately supported; response is generally focused.	Organization is clear, though minor flaws may be present and some ideas may be disconnected.	Evidence is adequate and includes facts and details.	Ideas are adequately conveyed, using both precise and more general language; may include domain-specific vocabulary.	Command of conventions is sufficiently demonstrated.
2	Opinion is somewhat supported; response may lack focus or include unnecessary material.	Organization is inconsistent, and flaws are apparent.	Evidence is uneven or incomplete; insufficient use of facts and details.	Ideas are unevenly conveyed, using overly-simplistic language; lack of domain-specific vocabulary.	Command of conventions is uneven.
1	The response may be confusing, unfocused; opinion not sufficiently supported.	Organization is poor or nonexistent.	Evidence is poor or nonexistent.	Ideas are conveyed in a vague, unclear, or confusing manner.	There is very little command of conventions.
0	The response shows no evidence of the ability to construct a coherent opinion essay using information from sources.				

© **Common Core State Standards**

Writing 1. Write opinion pieces on topics or texts, supporting a point of view with reasons and information. **Writing 9.a.** Apply grade 5 Reading standards to literature (e.g., "Compare and contrast two or more characters, settings, or events in a story or a drama, drawing on specific details in the text [e.g., how characters interact]"). **Writing 9.b.** Apply grade 5 Reading standards to informational texts (e.g., "Explain how an author uses reasons and evidence to support particular points in a text, identifying which reasons and evidence support which point[s]").

Write Like a Reporter
Argumentative Paragraph

Student Prompt Reread *Leonardo's Horse* and then look at p. 374, which states that Leonardo da Vinci wrote "I have wasted my hours" in one of his notebooks. Do you agree or disagree with the artist's statement? Write a paragraph that states your opinion. Use facts and details from the text to support your claim. Use linking phrases, such as *for instance, in order to,* and *in addition,* to make your reasoning clear.

_____

_____

_____

_____

_____

_____

_____

_____

_____

_____

_____

_____

_____

_____

_____

_____

_____

_____

Write Like a Reporter
Argumentative Paragraph

Student Prompt, p. 74 Reread *Leonardo's Horse* and then look at p. 374, which states that Leonardo da Vinci wrote "I have wasted my hours" in one of his notebooks. Do you agree or disagree with the artist's statement? Write a paragraph that states your opinion. Use facts and details from the text to support your claim. Use linking phrases, such as *for instance, in order to,* and *in addition,* to make your reasoning clear.

Writing to Sources After students reread the story, discuss Leonardo da Vinci's contributions to the worlds of art and science. As students begin their responses, remind them to state an opinion. Guide them to use facts and details from the text to support their reasoning. Remind students to reread carefully and find relevant evidence from the text that supports their opinions. Also remind students to use linking phrases to clarify their reasoning.

Students' paragraphs should:

- clearly state an opinion
- provide reasons that are supported by facts and details from the text
- link opinion and reasons using phrases
- demonstrate strong command of the conventions of standard written English

Ⓒ **Common Core State Standards**

Writing 1. Write opinion pieces on topics or texts, supporting a point of view with reasons and information. **Writing 9.b.** Apply grade 5 Reading standards to informational texts (e.g., "Explain how an author uses reasons and evidence to support particular points in a text, identifying which reasons and evidence support which point[s]").

Connect the Texts
Argumentative Essay

Student Prompt Look back at *Leonardo's Horse* and "A Job for Michelangelo." Compare and contrast the information about both artists. Which one showed more dedication to achieving his goals? In a short essay, state your opinion. Use details and facts from both texts to support your claim. Group your ideas in an organizational structure that clarifies your opinion and support.

_____

_____

_____

_____

_____

_____

_____

_____

_____

_____

_____

_____

_____

_____

_____

_____

_____

_____

Connect the Texts
Argumentative Essay

Student Prompt, p. 76 Look back at *Leonardo's Horse* and "A Job for Michelangelo." Compare and contrast the information about both artists. Which one showed more dedication to achieving his goals? In a short essay, state your opinion. Use details and facts from both texts to support your claim. Group your ideas in an organizational structure that clarifies your opinion and support.

Writing to Sources After students reread the historical fiction texts, discuss their opinions about Leonardo da Vinci and Michelangelo. Then discuss each artist's drive and dedication. Guide students to consider what they know about the artists' characters, and have them determine which man was more successful. Students' responses should use relevant facts and details from both texts in an organizational structure that makes their reasoning clear.

4-point Argument Writing Rubric					
Score	**Statement of Purpose/Focus**	**Organization**	**Development of Evidence**	**Language and Vocabulary**	**Conventions**
4	Opinion is clearly conveyed and well supported; response is focused.	Organization is clear and effective, creating a sense of cohesion.	Evidence is thorough and persuasive, and includes facts and details.	Ideas are clearly and effectively conveyed, using precise language and/or domain-specific vocabulary.	Command of conventions is strongly demonstrated.
3	Opinion is clear, adequately supported; response is generally focused.	Organization is clear, though minor flaws may be present and some ideas may be disconnected.	Evidence is adequate and includes facts and details.	Ideas are adequately conveyed, using both precise and more general language; may include domain-specific vocabulary.	Command of conventions is sufficiently demonstrated.
2	Opinion is somewhat supported; response may lack focus or include unnecessary material.	Organization is inconsistent, and flaws are apparent.	Evidence is uneven or incomplete; insufficient use of facts and details.	Ideas are unevenly conveyed, using overly-simplistic language; lack of domain-specific vocabulary.	Command of conventions is uneven.
1	The response may be confusing, unfocused; opinion not sufficiently supported.	Organization is poor or nonexistent.	Evidence is poor or nonexistent.	Ideas are conveyed in a vague, unclear, or confusing manner.	There is very little command of conventions.
0	The response shows no evidence of the ability to construct a coherent opinion essay using information from sources.				

Ⓒ **Common Core State Standards**

Writing 1. Write opinion pieces on topics or texts, supporting a point of view with reasons and information. **Writing 9.a.** Apply grade 5 Reading standards to literature (e.g., "Compare and contrast two or more characters, settings, or events in a story or a drama, drawing on specific details in the text [e.g., how characters interact]"). **Writing 9.b.** Apply grade 5 Reading standards to informational texts (e.g., "Explain how an author uses reasons and evidence to support particular points in a text, identifying which reasons and evidence support which point[s]").

Write Like a Reporter
Argumentative Paragraph

> **Student Prompt** Reread the descriptions of how Waterhouse Hawkins builds dinosaur models on pp. 398–403. Then compare and contrast the illustrations on these pages. Which illustration best clarifies the information in the text? Write a paragraph that states your opinion. Support your opinion with relevant evidence, concrete details, and accurate descriptions and quotations. Conclude your paragraph with a sentence that summarizes your opinion.

_____

_____

_____

_____

_____

_____

_____

_____

_____

_____

_____

_____

_____

_____

_____

_____

Write Like a Reporter
Argumentative Paragraph

Student Prompt, p. 78 Reread the descriptions of how Waterhouse Hawkins builds dinosaur models on pp. 398–403. Then compare and contrast the illustrations on these pages. Which illustration best clarifies the information in the text? Write a paragraph that states your opinion. Support your opinion with relevant evidence, concrete details, and accurate descriptions and quotations. Conclude your paragraph with a sentence that summarizes your opinion.

Writing to Sources After students reread, ask them to focus on the details the author uses to describe the model dinosaur process and the information each illustration reveals or helps clarify. Before students write, remind them to support their opinions with relevant evidence, such as descriptions and quotations, and concrete details. Also remind them to end their paragraph with a convincing concluding sentence that summarizes their stance.

Students' paragraphs should:

- clearly state an opinion regarding which illustration best clarifies information in the text
- support the opinion with relevant evidence and concrete details
- provide a concluding statement that summarizes their argument
- demonstrate strong command of the conventions of standard written English

Ⓒ **Common Core State Standards**

Writing 1. Write opinion pieces on topics or texts, supporting a point of view with reasons and information. **Writing 9.b.** Apply grade 5 Reading standards to informational texts (e.g., "Explain how an author uses reasons and evidence to support particular points in a text, identifying which reasons and evidence support which point[s]").

Connect the Texts
Argumentative Paragraph

Student Prompt Look back at *The Dinosaurs of Waterhouse Hawkins* and "A Model Scientist." Based on your reading, which man shows more dedication to research before he builds his models? Write a paragraph that states your opinion with supporting details from both texts. Conclude your paragraph with a sentence that connects your reasons and your opinion.

_____

_____

_____

_____

_____

_____

_____

_____

_____

_____

_____

_____

_____

_____

_____

_____

Connect the Texts
Argumentative Paragraph

Student Prompt, p. 80 Look back at *The Dinosaurs of Waterhouse Hawkins* and "A Model Scientist." Based on your reading, which man shows more dedication to research before he builds his models? Write a paragraph that states your opinion with supporting details from both texts. Conclude your paragraph with a sentence that connects your reasons and your opinion.

Writing to Sources After students reread the biography and the interview, have them discuss which scientist is more dedicated to research. Then have each student write a paragraph that states his or her opinion using details, such as quotations and facts, from both texts as support. Remind students to write a concluding sentence that connects their reasons and their opinion.

\	\	\	\	\	\
4-point Argument Writing Rubric					
Score	**Statement of Purpose/Focus**	**Organization**	**Development of Evidence**	**Language and Vocabulary**	**Conventions**
4	Opinion is clearly conveyed and well supported; response is focused.	Organization is clear and effective, creating a sense of cohesion.	Evidence is thorough and persuasive, and includes facts and details.	Ideas are clearly and effectively conveyed, using precise language and/or domain-specific vocabulary.	Command of conventions is strongly demonstrated.
3	Opinion is clear, adequately supported; response is generally focused.	Organization is clear, though minor flaws may be present and some ideas may be disconnected.	Evidence is adequate and includes facts and details.	Ideas are adequately conveyed, using both precise and more general language; may include domain-specific vocabulary.	Command of conventions is sufficiently demonstrated.
2	Opinion is somewhat supported; response may lack focus or include unnecessary material.	Organization is inconsistent, and flaws are apparent.	Evidence is uneven or incomplete; insufficient use of facts and details.	Ideas are unevenly conveyed, using overly-simplistic language; lack of domain-specific vocabulary.	Command of conventions is uneven.
1	The response may be confusing, unfocused; opinion not sufficiently supported.	Organization is poor or nonexistent.	Evidence is poor or nonexistent.	Ideas are conveyed in a vague, unclear, or confusing manner.	There is very little command of conventions.
0	The response shows no evidence of the ability to construct a coherent opinion essay using information from sources.				

Ⓒ Common Core State Standards

Writing 1. Write opinion pieces on topics or texts, supporting a point of view with reasons and information. **Writing 9.b.** Apply grade 5 Reading standards to informational texts (e.g., "Explain how an author uses reasons and evidence to support particular points in a text, identifying which reasons and evidence support which point[s]").

Write Like a Reporter
Argumentative Paragraph

Student Prompt As you reread *Mahalia Jackson*, list the sequence of events. Do you think the author proves that Mahalia Jackson "brought the blues feeling into church music"? Write a paragraph that states your opinion. Create an organizational structure that groups your reasons to support your point of view. Use concrete details from the text to support your opinion. Include linking words, such as *consequently* and *specifically*, to make connections between your opinion and your reasons.

_____

_____

_____

_____

_____

_____

_____

_____

_____

_____

_____

_____

_____

_____

_____

_____

Write Like a Reporter

Argumentative Paragraph

> **Student Prompt, p. 82** As you reread *Mahalia Jackson,* list the sequence of events. Do you think the author proves that Mahalia Jackson "brought the blues feeling into church music"? Write a paragraph that states your opinion. Create an organizational structure that groups your reasons to support your point of view. Use concrete details from the text to support your opinion. Include linking words, such as *consequently* and *specifically*, to make connections between your opinion and your reasons.

Writing to Sources After students reread the expository text, have them list the main events. Students should examine the text for evidence of Mahalia Jackson incorporating the blues into her gospel music. Remind them to base their opinions on concrete details. Also remind students to establish an effective organizational structure to support their opinion and to use linking words and phrases to make sure their paragraphs are clearly organized.

Students' paragraphs should:

- create an organizational structure in which related ideas are grouped to support the writer's purpose
- provide reasons that are supported by details from the text
- link opinion and reasons using words related to the presented opinion
- demonstrate strong command of the conventions of standard written English

Ⓒ **Common Core State Standards**

Writing 1. Write opinion pieces on topics or texts, supporting a point of view with reasons and information. **Writing 9.b.** Apply grade 5 Reading standards to informational texts (e.g., "Explain how an author uses reasons and evidence to support particular points in a text, identifying which reasons and evidence support which point[s]").

Connect the Texts
Argumentative Paragraph

Student Prompt Reread *Mahalia Jackson* and the poems in "Perfect Harmony."
Compare and contrast how the speakers or narrators describe singing. Which text best
describes how it feels to sing? Write your opinion in a paragraph. Use concrete details,
including quotations, from the expository text and the poems to support your opinion. Use
linking words and phrases to make your reasoning clear.

_____

_____

_____

_____

_____

_____

_____

_____

_____

_____

_____

_____

_____

_____

_____

_____

_____

_____

_____

Connect the Texts
Argumentative Paragraph

Student Prompt, p. 84 Reread *Mahalia Jackson* and the poems in "Perfect Harmony." Compare and contrast how the speakers or narrators describe singing. Which text best describes how it feels to sing? Write your opinion in a paragraph. Use concrete details, including quotations, from the expository text and the poems to support your opinion. Use linking words and phrases to make your reasoning clear.

Writing to Sources After students reread the selection and the poems, have them point out descriptive details in the texts. Ask them to write a paragraph stating their opinion about which text best describes what it feels like to sing. Students should include quotations from each text as evidence to support their opinions. Remind students to use linking words and phrases to clarify their arguments.

4-point Argument Writing Rubric				
Score	Statement of Purpose/Focus	Organization	Development of Evidence	Language and Vocabulary	Conventions
4	Opinion is clearly conveyed and well supported; response is focused.	Organization is clear and effective, creating a sense of cohesion.	Evidence is thorough and persuasive, and includes facts and details.	Ideas are clearly and effectively conveyed, using precise language and/or domain-specific vocabulary.	Command of conventions is strongly demonstrated.
3	Opinion is clear, adequately supported; response is generally focused.	Organization is clear, though minor flaws may be present and some ideas may be disconnected.	Evidence is adequate and includes facts and details.	Ideas are adequately conveyed, using both precise and more general language; may include domain-specific vocabulary.	Command of conventions is sufficiently demonstrated.
2	Opinion is somewhat supported; response may lack focus or include unnecessary material.	Organization is inconsistent, and flaws are apparent.	Evidence is uneven or incomplete; insufficient use of facts and details.	Ideas are unevenly conveyed, using overly-simplistic language; lack of domain-specific vocabulary.	Command of conventions is uneven.
1	The response may be confusing, unfocused; opinion not sufficiently supported.	Organization is poor or nonexistent.	Evidence is poor or nonexistent.	Ideas are conveyed in a vague, unclear, or confusing manner.	There is very little command of conventions.
0	The response shows no evidence of the ability to construct a coherent opinion essay using information from sources.				

Ⓒ **Common Core State Standards**

Writing 1. Write opinion pieces on topics or texts, supporting a point of view with reasons and information. **Writing 9.a.** Apply grade 5 Reading standards to literature (e.g., "Compare and contrast two or more characters, settings, or events in a story or a drama, drawing on specific details in the text [e.g., how characters interact]"). **Writing 9.b.** Apply grade 5 Reading standards to informational texts (e.g., "Explain how an author uses reasons and evidence to support particular points in a text, identifying which reasons and evidence support which point[s]").

Write Like a Reporter
Argumentative Paragraph

Student Prompt Reread *Special Effects in Film and Television* and make careful notes on the text's facts and details. In your opinion, which two steps in the miniature model-making process are the most important? Write a paragraph that states your opinion, and support your claim with reasons and details from the text. Use linking phrases, such as *for instance, in order to,* and *in addition,* to make your reasoning clear.

_____

_____

_____

_____

_____

_____

_____

_____

_____

_____

_____

_____

_____

_____

_____

_____

_____

_____

_____

Write Like a Reporter
Argumentative Paragraph

Student Prompt, p. 86 Reread *Special Effects in Film and Television* and make careful notes on the text's facts and details. In your opinion, which two steps in the miniature model-making process are the most important? Write a paragraph that states your opinion, and support your claim with reasons and details from the text. Use linking phrases, such as *for instance, in order to,* and *in addition,* to make your reasoning clear.

Writing to Sources After students reread *Special Effects in Film and Television,* ask them to list the details that relate to the building of miniature models. Each student should choose the two steps he or she believes are most important in the miniature model-making process. Guide students to clearly state their opinions and support them with evidence from the text. Remind students to use linking phrases to clarify their opinions.

Students' paragraphs should:

- clearly state an opinion regarding the events of the text
- support the opinion with relevant evidence
- link opinion and reasons using phrases
- demonstrate strong command of the conventions of standard written English

Ⓒ **Common Core State Standards**

Writing 1. Write opinion pieces on topics or texts, supporting a point of view with reasons and information. **Writing 9.b.** Apply grade 5 Reading standards to informational texts (e.g., "Explain how an author uses reasons and evidence to support particular points in a text, identifying which reasons and evidence support which point[s]").

Connect the Texts
Argumentative Paragraph

Student Prompt Reread *Special Effects in Film and Television* and the online article "Searching for Animation." In your opinion, after reading the longer text, did the online source give you useful new information about special effects? In one paragraph, state your opinion, give reasons, and use facts and details from both texts to support your reasons. Conclude your paragraph with a sentence that clarifies your opinion.

_____

_____

_____

_____

_____

_____

_____

_____

_____

_____

_____

_____

_____

_____

_____

_____

_____

_____

Connect the Texts
Argumentative Paragraph

> **Student Prompt, p. 88** Reread *Special Effects in Film and Television* and the online article "Searching for Animation." In your opinion, after reading the longer text, did the online source give you useful new information about special effects? In one paragraph, state your opinion, give reasons, and use facts and details from both texts to support your reasons. Conclude your paragraph with a sentence that clarifies your opinion.

Writing to Sources After students reread *Special Effects in Film and Television*, the instruction on how to use a search engine, and information from the online article, ask them to point out the main facts in each passage. Have them write a paragraph that states their opinion about whether the article from the Web site gave useful new information about special effects. Students should include evidence from each text to support their opinions. Ask them to include a concluding sentence that summarizes their opinions.

	4-point Argument Writing Rubric				
Score	**Statement of Purpose/Focus**	**Organization**	**Development of Evidence**	**Language and Vocabulary**	**Conventions**
4	Opinion is clearly conveyed and well supported; response is focused.	Organization is clear and effective, creating a sense of cohesion.	Evidence is thorough and persuasive, and includes facts and details.	Ideas are clearly and effectively conveyed, using precise language and/or domain-specific vocabulary.	Command of conventions is strongly demonstrated.
3	Opinion is clear, adequately supported; response is generally focused.	Organization is clear, though minor flaws may be present and some ideas may be disconnected.	Evidence is adequate and includes facts and details.	Ideas are adequately conveyed, using both precise and more general language; may include domain-specific vocabulary.	Command of conventions is sufficiently demonstrated.
2	Opinion is somewhat supported; response may lack focus or include unnecessary material.	Organization is inconsistent, and flaws are apparent.	Evidence is uneven or incomplete; insufficient use of facts and details.	Ideas are unevenly conveyed, using overly-simplistic language; lack of domain-specific vocabulary.	Command of conventions is uneven.
1	The response may be confusing, unfocused; opinion not sufficiently supported.	Organization is poor or nonexistent.	Evidence is poor or nonexistent.	Ideas are conveyed in a vague, unclear, or confusing manner.	There is very little command of conventions.
0	The response shows no evidence of the ability to construct a coherent opinion essay using information from sources.				

© Common Core State Standards

Writing 1. Write opinion pieces on topics or texts, supporting a point of view with reasons and information. **Writing 9.b.** Apply grade 5 Reading standards to informational texts (e.g., "Explain how an author uses reasons and evidence to support particular points in a text, identifying which reasons and evidence support which point[s]").

Prove It!
Argumentative Essay

Academic Vocabulary

An **argument** is persuasive writing that states a writer's opinion about a topic and develops an argument using reasons that are supported by facts and examples.

ELL

Introduce Genre Write *opinion* on the board. Explain that an opinion cannot be proved true or false. It is a statement of belief. Point out that an argument is based on the author's opinion about a topic.

Artists and Inventors

Argumentative Essay

In this unit, students have read examples of argumentative writing and have had the opportunity to write in this mode. Remind students of texts and writing tasks (such as Write Like a Reporter and Connect the Texts) in which they have encountered and practiced argumentative writing.

Key Features of an Argumentative Essay

- states an opinion, or claim, on a topic
- includes sound reasoning and relevant evidence, such as facts and details, to support the claim
- organizes reasons in a clear and logical order
- includes transition words, phrases, and clauses to link reasons to the opinion
- has an introduction, body, and conclusion

Writing Task Overview

Each unit writing task provides students with an opportunity to write to sources. To successfully complete the task, students must analyze, synthesize, and evaluate multiple complex texts and create their own written response.

Artists and Inventors

Part 1: Students will reread and take notes on the selected sources. They will then respond to several questions about these sources and discuss their written responses with partners or in small groups.

Part 2: Students will work individually to plan, write, and revise their own argumentative essay.

Scorable Products: short responses, argumentative essay

Artists and Inventors: Writing Task – Short Response

Teacher Directions:

1. **Introduce the Sources** Refer students to the following texts in the Student Edition:

   1. *Leonardo's Horse,* pp. 360–377

   2. *The Dinosaurs of Waterhouse Hawkins,* pp. 394–411

   3. *Mahalia Jackson*, pp. 430–437

   Explain to students that they will need to draw evidence and support from the texts above in order to answer evidence-based short response questions and to write an argumentative essay. Students should take notes and categorize information as they closely reread the texts. Students should be given paper or a relevant graphic organizer from the TR DVD for note-taking.

2. **Provide Student Directions and Scoring Information (p. 94)** Answer any task-related questions students may have. If necessary, provide additional paper for students to write their responses.

3. **Initiate the Writing Task** If you are timing this part of the task, you may wish to alert students when half the allotted time has elapsed and again when 5 minutes remain.

4. **Facilitate Collaboration** After students have completed their written responses to the evidence-based short response questions, assign partners or small groups and have them discuss their responses. If students struggle to work together productively, provide them with tips and strategies for expressing their ideas and commenting on the ideas of others.

ⓒ Common Core State Standards

Writing 1. Write opinion pieces on topics or texts, supporting a point of view with reasons and information. **Speaking/Listening 1.** Engage effectively in a range of collaborative discussions (one-on-one, in groups, and teacher-led) with diverse partners on grade 5 topics and texts, building on others' ideas and expressing their own clearly. **(Also Writing 1.a., Writing 1.b., Writing 1.c., Writing 1.d., Writing 1.d.)**

Scoring Information

Use the following 2-point scoring rubrics to evaluate students' answers to the evidence-based short response questions.

1. Using details from the texts, identify and compare one major achievement of Leonardo da Vinci, Waterhouse Hawkins, and Mahalia Jackson.

	Analysis Rubric
2	The response: • demonstrates the ability to analyze similarities and differences between the texts • includes specific details that make reference to the texts
1	The response: • demonstrates a limited ability to analyze similarities and differences between the texts • includes some details that make reference to the texts
0	A response receives no credit if it demonstrates no ability to analyze similarities and differences between the texts or includes no relevant details from the texts.

2. Draw conclusions about why Leonardo da Vinci, Waterhouse Hawkins, and Mahalia Jackson viewed their personal achievements so differently. Identify key words and phrases the authors use in their descriptions to draw your conclusions.

	Synthesis Rubric
2	The response: • demonstrates the ability to synthesize information from the sources in order to draw an overall conclusion • includes specific details that make reference to the texts
1	The response: • demonstrates a limited ability to synthesize information from the sources in order to draw an overall conclusion • includes some details that make reference to the texts
0	A response receives no credit if it demonstrates no ability to synthesize information from the sources or includes no relevant details from the texts.

3. Evaluate whether art and inventions are necessary to inspire new ideas from others. Use details from each text to support your answer.

Evaluation Rubric	
2	The response: • demonstrates the ability to evaluate themes and ideas from texts • includes specific details that make reference to the texts
1	The response: • demonstrates a limited ability to evaluate themes and ideas from texts • includes some details that make reference to the texts
0	A response receives no credit if it demonstrates no ability to evaluate information from the sources or includes no relevant details from the texts.

© **Common Core State Standards**

Writing 8. Recall relevant information from experiences or gather relevant information from print and digital sources; summarize or paraphrase information in notes and finished work, and provide a list of sources. **Writing 9.** Draw evidence from literary or informational texts to support analysis, reflection, and research.

Artists and Inventors
Writing Task – Short Response

Student Directions:

Your Assignment You will reread several selections from Unit 3 and take notes on these sources. Then you will answer three questions about these materials. You may refer to your notes or to any of the sources as often as you like.

Sources

1. *Leonardo's Horse,* pp. 360–377

2. *The Dinosaurs of Waterhouse Hawkins,* pp. 394–411

3. *Mahalia Jackson,* pp. 430–437

Be sure to read closely and take good notes. Your sources and notes will be the basis for writing your own argumentative essay in the second half of this writing task.

Evidence-Based Short Response Questions Answer the short response questions on the lines provided below each question. Your answers to these questions will be scored. Be sure to base your answers on the sources you have just read. Remember that you may refer back to your notes or to any of the sources.

After you have answered the questions, you will discuss your responses with a partner. Your teacher will let you know when to begin the discussion part of this task.

Scoring Information Your responses will be scored based on how you demonstrate the ability to:

- compare information across texts
- include relevant evidence from the sources as support
- analyze, synthesize, and evaluate information
- distinguish key details from unnecessary information

Evidence-Based Short Response Questions

1. Using details from the texts, identify and compare one major achievement of Leonardo da Vinci, Waterhouse Hawkins, and Mahalia Jackson.

_____

_____

_____

_____

_____

2. Draw conclusions about why Leonardo da Vinci, Waterhouse Hawkins, and Mahalia Jackson viewed their personal achievements so differently. Identify key words and phrases the authors use in their descriptions to draw your conclusions.

_____

_____

_____

_____

_____

2. Evaluate whether art and inventions are necessary to inspire new ideas from others. Use details from each text to support your answer.

_____

_____

_____

_____

_____

Collaborative Discussion

After you have written your responses to the questions, discuss your ideas. Your teacher will assign you a partner and let you know when to begin.

Artists and Inventors: Writing Task – Argumentative Essay

Teacher Directions:

1. **Provide Student Directions and Scoring Information (p. 98)** Explain to students that they will now review their notes and sources, and plan, draft, and revise their argumentative essays. Although they may use their notes and sources, they must work alone. Students will be allowed to look back at the answers they wrote to the short response questions, but they will not be allowed to make changes to those answers. Have students read the directions for the argumentative essay and answer any task-related questions they may have. Students should be given paper on which to write their argumentative essays.

2. **Initiate the Writing Task** If you are timing this part of the task, you may wish to suggest approximate times for students to begin writing and revising. If students wish to continue writing rather than revising, allow them to do so. Alert students when 5 minutes remain.

3. **Scoring Information** Use the scoring rubric on the next page to evaluate students' argumentative essays.

4. **Essay Prompt** Use what you have learned from reading *Leonardo's Horse, The Dinosaurs of Waterhouse Hawkins,* and *Mahalia Jackson* to write an argumentative essay. State your opinion about why the work of artists and inventors is important for others, supporting your opinion with details from the three texts. Be sure to follow the conventions of written English.

4-point Argument Writing Rubric					
Score	Statement of Purpose/Focus	Organization	Development of Evidence	Language and Vocabulary	Conventions
4	Opinion is clearly conveyed and well supported; argument is focused.	Organization is clear and effective, creating a sense of cohesion.	Evidence is thorough and persuasive, and includes facts and details.	Ideas are clearly and effectively conveyed, using precise language and domain-specific vocabulary.	Command of conventions is strongly demonstrated.
3	Opinion is clear, adequately supported; argument is generally focused.	Organization is clear, though minor flaws may be present and some ideas may be disconnected.	Evidence is adequate and includes facts and details.	Ideas are adequately conveyed, using both precise and more general language; may include domain-specific vocabulary.	Command of conventions is sufficiently demonstrated.
2	Argument is somewhat supported; lacks focus or includes unnecessary material.	Organization is inconsistent, and flaws are apparent.	Evidence is uneven or incomplete; insufficient use of facts and details.	Ideas are unevenly conveyed, using simplistic language; lacks domain-specific vocabulary.	Command of conventions is uneven.
1	Argument is confusing, unfocused; opinion is not sufficiently supported.	Organization is poor or nonexistent.	Evidence is poor or nonexistent.	Ideas are conveyed in a vague, unclear, or confusing manner.	There is very little command of conventions.
0	The response shows no evidence of the ability to construct a coherent argumentative essay using information from sources.				

Ⓒ Common Core State Standards

Writing 1. Write opinion pieces on topics or texts, supporting a point of view with reasons and information. **Writing 9.** Draw evidence from literary or informational texts to support analysis, reflection, and research. **(Also Writing 1.a., Writing 1.b., Writing 10.)**

Artists and Inventors
Writing Task – Argumentative Essay

Student Directions:

Your Assignment Now you will review your notes and sources, and plan, draft, and revise your argumentative essay. While you may use your notes and refer to the sources, you must work on your own. You may also refer to the answers you wrote to earlier questions, but you cannot change those answers.

Argumentative Essay Prompt Use what you have learned from reading *Leonardo's Horse, The Dinosaurs of Waterhouse Hawkins,* and *Mahalia Jackson* to write an argumentative essay. State your opinion about why the work of artists and inventors is important for others, supporting your opinion with details from the three texts. Be sure to follow the conventions of written English.

Scoring Information Your argumentative essay will be assigned a score for

1. **Focus–** how clearly you introduce your topic and state your opinion
2. **Organization–** how well your essay groups related ideas together and explains the reasons in a logical order
3. **Elaboration–** how well you provide sound reasoning supported by facts and details
4. **Language and Vocabulary–** how well you use words, phrases, and clauses to link your opinion and reasons and whether your language is precise
5. **Conventions–** how well you follow the rules of grammar, usage, capitalization, punctuation, and spelling

Now begin work on your argumentative essay. Try to manage your time carefully so that you can

- plan your argumentative essay
- write your argumentative essay
- revise and edit for a final draft

Artists and Inventors: Writing Task – Argumentative Essay

Teacher Directions:

1. Publish Explain to students that publishing their writing is the last step in the writing process. If time permits, have students review one another's compositions and incorporate any comments their classmates have. Offer students suggestions for how to publish their work, such as in a school newspaper, brochure, or blog post. Encourage students to use the Internet to share their work with others.

2. Present Students will now have the option to present their arguments. Have students give debates on their argumentative essays in front of the class. Use the list below to offer students some tips on listening and speaking.

While Listening to a Classmate...

- Face the speaker to listen attentively.
- Take notes on what the speaker says.

While Speaking to Classmates...

- Have good posture and eye contact.
- Speak clearly and at an appropriate pace.
- Keep in mind your purpose for speaking.

Things to Do Together...

- Ask and answer questions with detail.
- Clarify or follow up on information presented.
- Contribute to the discussion and expand on each other's ideas.

© Common Core State Standards

Writing 6. With some guidance and support from adults, use technology, including the Internet, to produce and publish writing as well as to interact and collaborate with others; demonstrate sufficient command of keyboarding skills to type a minimum of two pages in a single sitting. **Speaking/Listening 1.b.** Follow agreed-upon rules for discussions and carry out assigned roles. **Speaking/Listening 1.c.** Pose and respond to specific questions by making comments that contribute to the discussion and elaborate on the remarks of others. **Speaking/Listening 4.** Report on a topic or text or present an opinion, sequencing ideas logically and using appropriate facts and relevant, descriptive details to support main ideas or themes; speak clearly at an understandable pace.

Unit 4 Adapting

Writing Focus: Informative/Explanatory

Write Like a Reporter

Informative/Explanatory Paragraph

Student Prompt Reread the story on pp. 32–37 and summarize the things Wesley makes from "swist." Then write a one-paragraph explanation that tells how Wesley uses the plant to create his civilization, Weslandia. Use concrete details, such as facts and examples, from the text to explain what makes up Wesley's civilization. Include linking words and phrases, such as *in contrast* and *especially*, to make your explanation clear. Conclude your paragraph with a statement that summarizes your explanation.

_____

_____

_____

_____

_____

_____

_____

_____

_____

_____

_____

_____

_____

_____

_____

Write Like a Reporter

Informative/Explanatory Paragraph

Student Prompt, p. 102 Reread the story on pp. 32–37 and summarize the things Wesley makes from "swist." Then write a one-paragraph explanation that tells how Wesley uses the plant to create his civilization, Weslandia. Use concrete details, such as facts and examples, from the text to explain what makes up Wesley's civilization. Include linking words and phrases, such as *in contrast* and *especially,* to make your explanation clear. Conclude your paragraph with a statement that summarizes your explanation.

Writing to Sources After students reread the passage, have them make a list of every use Wesley has for swist. Before students begin writing, have them consider how Wesley creates Weslandia from the items he makes out of swist. Remind them to clearly explain how Wesley uses the different items to build his civilization. Students should include specific text details in their explanations and use linking words and phrases to show the relationships between their ideas. Remind them to end with a concluding sentence that sums up their explanation.

Students' paragraphs should:

- clearly introduce specific information about how the character builds a civilization
- develop the topic with concrete details and facts from the text
- use linking words and phrases to show the relationships between ideas
- demonstrate strong command of the conventions of standard written English

Ⓒ **Common Core State Standards**

Writing 2. Write informative/explanatory texts to examine a topic and convey ideas and information clearly. **Writing 9.a.** Apply grade 5 Reading standards to literature (e.g., "Compare and contrast two or more characters, settings, or events in a story or a drama, drawing on specific details in the text [e.g., how characters interact]").

Connect the Texts

Informative/Explanatory Essay

Student Prompt Look back at *Weslandia*, "Under the Back Porch," and "Keziah." Find evidence that explains why Wesley and the poems' speakers want their own special places. Then write a short explanatory essay that compares and contrasts the speakers' and character's perspectives and the challenges they face in finding their special places. Include details and imagery from all three texts to support your explanation.

_____

_____

_____

_____

_____

_____

_____

_____

_____

_____

_____

_____

_____

_____

_____

_____

_____

Connect the Texts
Informative/Explanatory Essay

Student Prompt, p. 104 Look back at *Weslandia*, "Under the Back Porch," and "Keziah." Find evidence that explains why Wesley and the poems' speakers want their own special places. Then write a short explanatory essay that compares and contrasts the speakers' and character's perspectives and the challenges they face in finding their special places. Include details and imagery from all three texts to support your explanation.

Writing to Sources Have students reread the texts. Then have them summarize why the character or speaker in each text wants a special place, based on textual evidence such as examples and descriptive details. As they write their explanatory paragraphs, students should compare and contrast the character and the speakers in the texts. Check that students' ideas are organized logically and that they use linking words and phrases to make their explanations clear.

Informative/Explanatory Writing Rubric					
Score	Focus	Organization	Development of Evidence	Language and Vocabulary	Conventions
4	Main idea is clearly conveyed and well supported; response is focused.	Organization is clear and effective, creating a sense of cohesion.	Evidence is relevant and thorough; includes facts and details.	Ideas are clearly and effectively conveyed, using precise language and/or domain-specific vocabulary.	Command of conventions is strongly demonstrated.
3	Main idea is clear, adequately supported; response is generally focused.	Organization is clear, though minor flaws may be present and some ideas may be disconnected.	Evidence is adequate and includes facts and details.	Ideas are adequately conveyed, using both precise and more general language; may include domain-specific vocabulary.	Command of conventions is sufficiently demonstrated.
2	Main idea is somewhat supported; lacks focus or includes unnecessary material.	Organization is inconsistent, and flaws are apparent.	Evidence is uneven or incomplete; insufficient use of facts and details.	Ideas are unevenly conveyed, using overly-simplistic language; lacks domain-specific vocabulary.	Command of conventions is uneven.
1	Response may be confusing, unfocused; main idea insufficiently supported.	Organization is poor or nonexistent.	Evidence is poor or nonexistent.	Ideas are conveyed in a vague, unclear, or confusing manner.	There is very little command of conventions.
0	The response shows no evidence of the ability to construct a coherent explanatory essay using information from sources.				

Ⓒ Common Core State Standards

Writing 2. Write informative/explanatory texts to examine a topic and convey ideas and information clearly. **Writing 9.a.** Apply grade 5 Reading standards to literature (e.g., "Compare and contrast two or more characters, settings, or events in a story or a drama, drawing on specific details in the text [e.g., how characters interact]").

Write Like a Reporter
Informative/Explanatory Paragraph

> **Student Prompt** Reread *Tripping Over the Lunch Lady* on pp. 52–67 and focus on the illustrations. Take notes on how the illustrations correspond to different parts of the story. Then write a one-paragraph explanation that focuses on how the illustrations contribute to the meaning and tone of the text. Support your explanation with examples from the text, including concrete details and precise language that describes the illustrations.

_____

_____

_____

_____

_____

_____

_____

_____

_____

_____

_____

_____

_____

_____

_____

_____

_____

_____

Write Like a Reporter
Informative/Explanatory Paragraph

Student Prompt, p. 106 Reread *Tripping Over the Lunch Lady* on pp. 52–67 and focus on the illustrations. Take notes on how the illustrations correspond with different parts of the story. Then write a one-paragraph explanation that focuses on how the illustrations contribute to the meaning and tone of the text. Support your explanation with examples from the text, including concrete details and precise language that describes the illustrations.

Writing to Sources As student reread *Tripping Over the Lunch Lady,* have them locate the specific parts of the text that correspond to the illustrations. In their explanations, students should use concrete words, phrases, and details from the text to help explain what the illustrations depict and why those moments were highlighted. Students should then analyze how the illustrations contribute to the meaning and tone of the text. Remind students to reread the text carefully and base their responses on details from the original story.

Students' paragraphs should:

- clearly introduce specific information about how the illustrations relate to meaning and tone
- develop the topic with specific examples and concrete details from the text
- use precise language to describe the illustrations
- demonstrate strong command of the conventions of standard written English

© **Common Core State Standards**

Writing 2. Write informative/explanatory texts to examine a topic and convey ideas and information clearly. **Writing 9.a.** Apply grade 5 Reading standards to literature (e.g., "Compare and contrast two or more characters, settings, or events in a story or a drama, drawing on specific details in the text [e.g., how characters interact]").

Connect the Texts
Informative/Explanatory Essay

> **Student Prompt** Look back at *Tripping Over the Lunch Lady* and "Square Dancing: Good for the Heart and Mind." Why do Jinx and Victoria Barrett think square dancing is a good activity? Write a short explanatory essay comparing and contrasting the information in "Square Dancing" with Jinx's experience square dancing with Josh. Carefully reread both texts to find facts, concrete details, and accurate quotations to support your explanation.

_____

_____

_____

_____

_____

_____

_____

_____

_____

_____

_____

_____

_____

_____

_____

_____

_____

Connect the Texts
Informative/Explanatory Essay

Student Prompt, p. 108 Look back at *Tripping Over the Lunch Lady* and "Square Dancing: Good for the Heart and Mind." Why do Jinx and Victoria Barrett think square dancing is a good activity? Write a short explanatory essay comparing and contrasting the information in "Square Dancing" with Jinx's experience square dancing with Josh. Carefully reread both texts to find facts, concrete details, and accurate quotations to support your explanation.

Writing to Sources Discuss with students how *Tripping Over the Lunch Lady* and "Square Dancing: Good for the Heart and Mind" present reasons supporting the benefits of square dancing. Then have them carefully reread the story and the persuasive text to find specific facts and details. Remind them to include accurate quotations, concrete details, and facts to support their explanations.

	Informative/Explanatory Writing Rubric				
Score	**Focus**	**Organization**	**Development of Evidence**	**Language and Vocabulary**	**Conventions**
4	Main idea is clearly conveyed and well supported; response is focused.	Organization is clear and effective, creating a sense of cohesion.	Evidence is relevant and thorough; includes facts and details.	Ideas are clearly and effectively conveyed, using precise language and/or domain-specific vocabulary.	Command of conventions is strongly demonstrated.
3	Main idea is clear, adequately supported; response is generally focused.	Organization is clear, though minor flaws may be present and some ideas may be disconnected.	Evidence is adequate and includes facts and details.	Ideas are adequately conveyed, using both precise and more general language; may include domain-specific vocabulary.	Command of conventions is sufficiently demonstrated.
2	Main idea is somewhat supported; lacks focus or includes unnecessary material.	Organization is inconsistent, and flaws are apparent.	Evidence is uneven or incomplete; insufficient use of facts and details.	Ideas are unevenly conveyed, using overly-simplistic language; lacks domain-specific vocabulary.	Command of conventions is uneven.
1	Response may be confusing, unfocused; main idea insufficiently supported.	Organization is poor or nonexistent.	Evidence is poor or nonexistent.	Ideas are conveyed in a vague, unclear, or confusing manner.	There is very little command of conventions.
0	The response shows no evidence of the ability to construct a coherent explanatory essay using information from sources.				

Writing 2. Write informative/explanatory texts to examine a topic and convey ideas and information clearly. **Writing 9.a.** Apply grade 5 Reading standards to literature (e.g., "Compare and contrast two or more characters, settings, or events in a story or a drama, drawing on specific details in the text [e.g., how characters interact]"). **Writing 9.b.** Apply grade 5 Reading standards to informational texts (e.g., "Explain how an author uses reasons and evidence to support particular points in a text, identifying which reasons and evidence support which point[s]").

Write Like a Reporter
Informative/Explanatory Paragraph

> **Student Prompt** Reread the information on ants on pp. 86–89. Write down the main ideas, and make a list of the evidence Joanne Settel uses to support these particular points. Then write a paragraph that explains how the structure of the section helps readers process the information. Include examples of technical vocabulary and concrete details based on the original text. Also include accurate quotations and facts to support your explanation.

_____

_____

_____

_____

_____

_____

_____

_____

_____

_____

_____

_____

_____

_____

_____

_____

_____

_____

Write Like a Reporter
Informative/Explanatory Paragraph

Student Prompt, p. 110 Reread the information on ants on pp. 86–89. Write down the main ideas, and make a list of evidence Joanne Settel uses to support these particular points. Then write a paragraph that explains how the structure of the section helps readers process the information. Include examples of technical vocabulary and concrete details based on the original text. Also include accurate quotations and facts to support your explanation.

Writing to Sources As students reread *Exploding Ants*, have them pay particular attention to its structure. Before they begin writing, remind them that the author breaks the information into subsections instead of lumping it together. Students should also note any technical vocabulary or specific language they learned from the text. Remind students to reread the text carefully and base their explanations on details from the original text.

Students' paragraphs should:

- clearly introduce specific information about the structure of the expository text
- develop the topic with facts and quotations from the text
- use domain-specific vocabulary to explain the topic
- demonstrate strong command of the conventions of standard written English

© **Common Core State Standards**

Writing 2. Write informative/explanatory texts to examine a topic and convey ideas and information clearly. **Writing 9.b.** Apply grade 5 Reading standards to informational texts (e.g., "Explain how an author uses reasons and evidence to support particular points in a text, identifying which reasons and evidence support which point[s]").

Connect the Texts
Informative/Explanatory Essay

Student Prompt Look back at *Exploding Ants* and "The Art of Mimicry." How do animals use their bodies in unusual ways? In a short explanatory essay, retell these facts from the texts in a new way. Use subheadings such as "Eating Habits" or "Defensive Strategies" to explain related information. Include linking words, such as *similarly* or *specifically*, to make your explanation clear. Carefully reread both texts to find facts, concrete details, and accurate quotations to support your explanation.

_____

_____

_____

_____

_____

_____

_____

_____

_____

_____

_____

_____

_____

_____

_____

_____

Connect the Texts
Informative/Explanatory Essay

Student Prompt, p. 112 Look back at *Exploding Ants* and "The Art of Mimicry." How do animals use their bodies in unusual ways? In a short explanatory essay, retell these facts from the texts in a new way. Use subheadings such as "Eating Habits" or "Defensive Strategies" to explain related information. Include linking words, such as *similarly* or *specifically,* to make your explanation clear. Carefully reread both texts to find facts, concrete details, and accurate quotations to support your explanation.

Writing to Sources Discuss with students how *Exploding Ants* and "The Art of Mimicry" both use an organizational structure that includes subsections to convey information. Then have students carefully reread the expository texts to find different categories based on the different ways animals use their bodies. Students should link ideas within and across categories of information using words. Students' essays should include quotations, concrete details, and facts from both texts to support their conclusions.

Informative/Explanatory Writing Rubric				
Score	**Focus**	**Organization**	**Development of Evidence**	**Language and Vocabulary**	**Conventions**
4	Main idea is clearly conveyed and well supported; response is focused.	Organization is clear and effective, creating a sense of cohesion.	Evidence is relevant and thorough; includes facts and details.	Ideas are clearly and effectively conveyed, using precise language and/or domain-specific vocabulary.	Command of conventions is strongly demonstrated.
3	Main idea is clear, adequately supported; response is generally focused.	Organization is clear, though minor flaws may be present and some ideas may be disconnected.	Evidence is adequate and includes facts and details.	Ideas are adequately conveyed, using both precise and more general language; may include domain-specific vocabulary.	Command of conventions is sufficiently demonstrated.
2	Main idea is somewhat supported; lacks focus or includes unnecessary material.	Organization is inconsistent, and flaws are apparent.	Evidence is uneven or incomplete; insufficient use of facts and details.	Ideas are unevenly conveyed, using overly-simplistic language; lacks domain-specific vocabulary.	Command of conventions is uneven.
1	Response may be confusing, unfocused; main idea insufficiently supported.	Organization is poor or nonexistent.	Evidence is poor or nonexistent.	Ideas are conveyed in a vague, unclear, or confusing manner.	There is very little command of conventions.
0	The response shows no evidence of the ability to construct a coherent explanatory essay using information from sources.				

© Common Core State Standards

Writing 2. Write informative/explanatory texts to examine a topic and convey ideas and information clearly. **Writing 9.b.** Apply grade 5 Reading standards to informational texts (e.g., "Explain how an author uses reasons and evidence to support particular points in a text, identifying which reasons and evidence support which point[s]").

Write Like a Reporter
Informative/Explanatory Paragraph

Student Prompt Reread the dialogue on pp. 113–114 and pp. 118–119 and focus on the conversations between Stormi and her parents. Then write a one-paragraph explanation that compares and contrasts Stormi's mom and dad. Use concrete details, such as specific dialogue, from the text to help you draw a conclusion about Stormi's relationship with her parents. Conclude your paragraph with a statement that summarizes your explanation.

_____

_____

_____

_____

_____

_____

_____

_____

_____

_____

_____

_____

_____

_____

_____

_____

Write Like a Reporter
Informative/Explanatory Paragraph

> **Student Prompt, p. 114** Reread the dialogue on pp. 113–114 and pp. 118–119 and focus on the conversations between Stormi and her parents. Then write a one-paragraph explanation that compares and contrasts Stormi's mom and dad. Use concrete details, such as specific dialogue, from the text to help you draw a conclusion about Stormi's relationship with her parents. Conclude your paragraph with a statement that summarizes your explanation.

Writing to Sources Before students begin their explanatory paragraphs, have them summarize these parts of the story, focusing on conversations between Stormi and her mother and Stormi and her father. In their explanations, students should draw on specific details in the text to compare and contrast these characters and their conversations. Then they should draw a conclusion about Stormi's relationship with her parents. Remind students to reread the text carefully and base their responses on details from the original story.

Students' paragraphs should:

- provide a general observation about the character's relationship with her parents
- develop the topic with concrete details and quotations from the characters' dialogue
- end with a concluding statement that summarizes the information
- demonstrate strong command of the conventions of standard written English

---

Ⓒ **Common Core State Standards**

Writing 2. Write informative/explanatory texts to examine a topic and convey ideas and information clearly. **Writing 9.a.** Apply grade 5 Reading standards to literature (e.g., "Compare and contrast two or more characters, settings, or events in a story or a drama, drawing on specific details in the text [e.g., how characters interact]").

Connect the Texts
Informative/Explanatory Essay

Student Prompt Look back at *The Stormi Giovanni Club* and "The Extra Credit Club." Find evidence that explains why Stormi and Eduardo Cabrera started their clubs and the purpose of each group. Then write a short explanatory essay that shows how the perspective of each founder influences the description of the club's events. Carefully reread both texts to find facts, concrete details, and accurate quotations to support your explanation.

_____

_____

_____

_____

_____

_____

_____

_____

_____

_____

_____

_____

_____

_____

_____

_____

Connect the Texts
Informative/Explanatory Essay

Student Prompt, p. 116 Look back at *The Stormi Giovanni Club* and "The Extra Credit Club." Find evidence that explains why Stormi and Eduardo Cabrera started their clubs and the purpose of each group. Then write a short explanatory essay that shows how the perspective of each founder influences the description of the club's events. Carefully reread both texts to find facts, concrete details, and accurate quotations to support your explanation.

Writing to Sources First have students reread the texts. Then discuss the purposes of Stormi's and Eduardo's clubs based on evidence in the texts such as examples and descriptive details. As they write their essays, make sure students explain Stormi's and Eduardo's perspectives and consider how these viewpoints relate to both clubs. Students' essays should include accurate quotations, concrete details, and facts from both texts to support their explanations.

	Informative/Explanatory Writing Rubric				
Score	Focus	Organization	Development of Evidence	Language and Vocabulary	Conventions
4	Main idea is clearly conveyed and well supported; response is focused.	Organization is clear and effective, creating a sense of cohesion.	Evidence is relevant and thorough; includes facts and details.	Ideas are clearly and effectively conveyed, using precise language and/or domain-specific vocabulary.	Command of conventions is strongly demonstrated.
3	Main idea is clear, adequately supported; response is generally focused.	Organization is clear, though minor flaws may be present and some ideas may be disconnected.	Evidence is adequate and includes facts and details.	Ideas are adequately conveyed, using both precise and more general language; may include domain-specific vocabulary.	Command of conventions is sufficiently demonstrated.
2	Main idea is somewhat supported; lacks focus or includes unnecessary material.	Organization is inconsistent, and flaws are apparent.	Evidence is uneven or incomplete; insufficient use of facts and details.	Ideas are unevenly conveyed, using overly-simplistic language; lacks domain-specific vocabulary.	Command of conventions is uneven.
1	Response may be confusing, unfocused; main idea insufficiently supported.	Organization is poor or nonexistent.	Evidence is poor or nonexistent.	Ideas are conveyed in a vague, unclear, or confusing manner.	There is very little command of conventions.
0	The response shows no evidence of the ability to construct a coherent explanatory essay using information from sources.				

© Common Core State Standards

Writing 2. Write informative/explanatory texts to examine a topic and convey ideas and information clearly. **Writing 9.a.** Apply grade 5 Reading standards to literature (e.g., "Compare and contrast two or more characters, settings, or events in a story or a drama, drawing on specific details in the text [e.g., how characters interact]"). **Writing 9.b.** Apply *grade 5 Reading standards* to informational texts (e.g., "Explain how an author uses reasons and evidence to support particular points in a text, identifying which reasons and evidence support which point[s]").

Write Like a Reporter
Informative/Explanatory Paragraph

Student Prompt Reread the autobiography on pp. 144–151 and focus on the key events regarding gymnastics. Create a list of the events in chronological order. Then write a paragraph that explains how the narrator's viewpoint toward the sport changes. Include transitions, such as *first, next,* and *then,* to show the chronology of events. Also include accurate quotations and concrete details based on the original text in your explanation.

_____

_____

_____

_____

_____

_____

_____

_____

_____

_____

_____

_____

_____

_____

_____

_____

Write Like a Reporter
Informative/Explanatory Paragraph

Student Prompt, p. 118 Reread the autobiography on pp. 144–151 and focus on the key events regarding gymnastics. Create a list of the events in chronological order. Then write a paragraph that explains how the narrator's viewpoint toward the sport changes. Include transitions, such as *first, next,* and *then,* to show the chronology of events. Also include accurate quotations and concrete details based on the original text in your explanation.

Writing to Sources As students reread the selection, have them list each of the key events regarding gymnastics in order. Before they begin writing, remind them that the chronology of events in their explanations must remain the same as in the autobiography. Remind students to use transitions to make the order clear. They should also include quotations and details to develop the explanation. Remind students to reread the text carefully and base their explanations on details from the original text.

Students' paragraphs should:

- provide a general observation about the narrator's viewpoint
- develop the topic with concrete details and quotations from the text
- link ideas using transitions that show the chronology of events
- demonstrate strong command of the conventions of standard written English

---

Ⓒ **Common Core State Standards**

Writing 2. Write informative/explanatory texts to examine a topic and convey ideas and information clearly. **Writing 9.b.** Apply grade 5 Reading standards to informational texts (e.g., "Explain how an author uses reasons and evidence to support particular points in a text, identifying which reasons and evidence support which point[s]").

Connect the Texts
Informative/Explanatory Essay

Student Prompt Look back at *The Gymnast* and "All About Gymnastics." Based on information from both texts, explain why gymnastics requires a lot of training. In a short explanatory essay, clarify the information from the online reference source for gymnastics and explain why the narrator of *The Gymnast* fails to complete a backflip. Carefully reread both texts to find facts, concrete details, and accurate quotations to support your explanation.

_____

_____

_____

_____

_____

_____

_____

_____

_____

_____

_____

_____

_____

_____

Connect the Texts
Informative/Explanatory Essay

> **Student Prompt, p. 120** Look back at *The Gymnast* and "All About Gymnastics." Based on information from both texts, explain why gymnastics requires a lot of training. In a short explanatory essay, clarify the information from the online reference sources for gymnastics and explain why the narrator of *The Gymnast* fails to complete a backflip. Carefully reread both texts to find facts, concrete details, and accurate quotations to support your explanation.

Writing to Sources Discuss with students how *The Gymnast* and "All About Gymnastics" present different information on gymnastics and its level of difficulty. Then have them carefully reread the autobiography and the online reference source to find specific facts and details. Student essays should include quotations, concrete details, and facts from the texts to support their conclusions.

Informative/Explanatory Writing Rubric					
Score	**Focus**	**Organization**	**Development of Evidence**	**Language and Vocabulary**	**Conventions**
4	Main idea is clearly conveyed and well supported; response is focused.	Organization is clear and effective, creating a sense of cohesion.	Evidence is relevant and thorough; includes facts and details.	Ideas are clearly and effectively conveyed, using precise language and/or domain-specific vocabulary.	Command of conventions is strongly demonstrated.
3	Main idea is clear, adequately supported; response is generally focused.	Organization is clear, though minor flaws may be present and some ideas may be disconnected.	Evidence is adequate and includes facts and details.	Ideas are adequately conveyed, using both precise and more general language; may include domain-specific vocabulary.	Command of conventions is sufficiently demonstrated.
2	Main idea is somewhat supported; lacks focus or includes unnecessary material.	Organization is inconsistent, and flaws are apparent.	Evidence is uneven or incomplete; insufficient use of facts and details.	Ideas are unevenly conveyed, using overly-simplistic language; lacks domain-specific vocabulary.	Command of conventions is uneven.
1	Response may be confusing, unfocused; main idea insufficiently supported.	Organization is poor or nonexistent.	Evidence is poor or nonexistent.	Ideas are conveyed in a vague, unclear, or confusing manner.	There is very little command of conventions.
0	The response shows no evidence of the ability to construct a coherent explanatory essay using information from sources.				

© Common Core State Standards

Writing 2. Write informative/explanatory texts to examine a topic and convey ideas and information clearly. **Writing 9.b.** Apply grade 5 Reading standards to informational texts (e.g., "Explain how an author uses reasons and evidence to support particular points in a text, identifying which reasons and evidence support which point[s]").

Prove It!
Informative/Explanatory Essay

Academic Vocabulary

A **cause** is something that makes an event happen. An **effect** is a result. In a **cause-and-effect text,** a writer explains causes, or effects, or how causes and effects are related. Often, each cause or effect is explained in a separate body paragraph.

ELL

Introduce Genre Write *cause and effect* on the board and place an arrow between them. Point out that a cause-and-effect essay shows how one thing leads to, or causes, another. Discuss with students the key features of a cause-and-effect text that appear on this page.

Cause for Change

Informative/Explanatory Cause-and-Effect Essay

In this unit, students have read examples of informative and explanatory writing, including a cause-and-effect article, and have had the opportunity to write in this mode. Remind students of texts and writing tasks (such as Write Like a Reporter and Connect the Texts) in which they have encountered and practiced informative/explanatory writing.

Key Features of an Informative/Explanatory Cause-and-Effect Essay

- focuses on and clearly explains the relationship between causes and effects
- develops the topic with facts, definitions, details, quotations, or other information
- includes transitional words, phrases, and clauses to link causes and effects
- uses precise language and domain-specific vocabulary
- provides a concluding statement or section related to the topic

Writing Task Overview

Each unit writing task provides students with an opportunity to write to sources. To successfully complete the task, students must analyze, synthesize, and evaluate multiple complex texts and create their own written response.

Cause for Change

Part 1: Students will read and take notes on the selected sources. They will then respond to several questions about these sources and discuss their written responses with partners or in small groups.

Part 2: Students will work individually to plan, write, and revise their own informative/explanatory cause-and-effect essay.

Scorable Products: evidence-based short responses, informative/explanatory cause-and-effect essay

Cause for Change: Writing Task – Short Response

Teacher Directions:

1. **Introduce the Sources** Refer students to the following texts in the Student Edition:

   1. *Weslandia,* pp. 26–37

   2. *The Stormi Giovanni Club,* pp. 110–125

   3. *The Gymnast,* pp. 142–151

   Explain to students that they will need to draw evidence and support from the texts above in order to answer evidence-based short response questions and to write an informative/explanatory cause-and-effect essay. Students should take notes and categorize information as they closely reread the texts. Students should be given paper or a relevant graphic organizer from the TR DVD for note-taking.

2. **Provide Student Directions and Scoring Information (p. 126)** Answer any task-related questions students may have. If necessary, provide additional paper for students to write their responses.

3. **Initiate the Writing Task** If you are timing this part of the task, you may wish to alert students when half the allotted time has elapsed and again when 5 minutes remain.

4. **Facilitate Collaboration** After students have completed their written responses to the evidence-based short response questions, assign partners and have them discuss their responses. If students struggle to work together productively, model questions and sentence starters that facilitate collaboration, such as: "Can you tell me more about ___ ?" and "I like ___. You could add ___."

© **Common Core State Standards**

Writing 2. Write informative/explanatory texts to examine a topic and convey ideas and information clearly. **Speaking/Listening 1.** Engage effectively in a range of collaborative discussions (one-on-one, in groups, and teacher-led) with diverse partners on grade 5 topics and texts, building on others' ideas and expressing their own clearly. **(Also Writing 2.a., Writing 2.b., Writing 2.c., Writing 2.d., Writing 2.e.)**

Scoring

Use the following 2-point scoring rubrics to evaluate students' answers to the evidence-based short response questions.

1. Identify the problems or conflicts that face the characters in the three stories. How are these problems alike and different? Include details from each text in your answer.

Analysis Rubric	
2	The response: • demonstrates the ability to analyze similarities and differences among the problems or conflicts • includes specific details that make reference to the texts
1	The response: • demonstrates a limited ability to analyze similarities and differences among the problems or conflicts • includes some details that make reference to the texts
0	A response receives no credit if it demonstrates no ability to analyze similarities and differences among the problems or conflicts or includes no relevant details from the texts.

2. In general, what effects do the problems or conflicts have on the characters? Cite examples and details from the texts about what the characters do to adapt.

Synthesis Rubric	
2	The response: • demonstrates the ability to synthesize information from the sources in order to identify effects • includes specific details that make reference to the texts
1	The response: • demonstrates a limited ability to synthesize information from the sources in order to identify effects • includes some details that make reference to the texts
0	A response receives no credit if it demonstrates no ability to synthesize information from the sources or includes no relevant details from the texts.

3. Rank the characters in order of *how well* they adapted. Cite examples from the texts that support your evaluation.

Evaluation Rubric	
2	The response: • demonstrates the ability to evaluate characters' responses • includes specific details that make reference to the texts
1	The response: • demonstrates a limited ability to evaluate characters' responses • includes some details that make reference to the texts
0	A response receives no credit if it demonstrates no ability to evaluate characters' responses or includes no relevant details from the texts.

ⓒ Common Core State Standards

Writing 8. Recall relevant information from experiences or gather relevant information from print and digital sources; summarize or paraphrase information in notes and finished work, and provide a list of sources. **Writing 9.** Draw evidence from literary or informational texts to support analysis, reflection, and research.

Cause for Change

Writing Task – Short Response

Student Directions:

Your Assignment You will reread several selections from Unit 4 and take notes on these sources. Then you will answer three questions about these texts. You may refer to your notes or to any of the sources as often as you like.

Sources

1. *Weslandia*, pp. 26–37

2. *The Stormi Giovanni Club*, pp. 110–125

3. *The Gymnast*, pp. 142–151

Be sure to read closely and take good notes. Your sources and notes will be the basis for writing your own cause-and-effect essay in the second half of this writing task.

Evidence-Based Short Response Questions Answer the short response questions on the lines provided below each question. Your answers to these questions will be scored. Be sure to base your answers on the sources you have just read. Remember that you may refer back to your notes or to any of the sources.

After you have answered the questions, you will discuss your responses with a partner or within a small group. Your teacher will let you know when to begin the discussion part of this task.

Scoring Information Your responses will be scored based on evidence of your ability to:

- compare and contrast information from multiple texts
- include relevant evidence from the sources
- identify, analyze, synthesize, and evaluate information from the sources
- distinguish key details and evidence from irrelevant information

Evidence-Based Short Response Questions

1. Identify the problems or conflicts that face the characters in the three stories. How are these problems alike and different? Include details from each text in your answer.

_____

_____

_____

_____

2. In general, what effects do the problems or conflicts have on the characters? Cite examples and details from the texts about what the characters do to adapt.

_____

_____

_____

_____

3. Rank the characters in order of *how well* they adapted. Cite examples from the texts that support your evaluation.

_____

_____

_____

_____

Collaborative Discussion

After you have written your responses to the questions, discuss your ideas. Your teacher will assign you a partner or a small group and let you know when to begin.

Cause for Change: Writing Task – Essay

Teacher Directions:

1. **Provide Student Directions and Scoring Information (p. 130)** Explain to students that they will now review their notes and sources, and plan, draft, and revise their cause-and-effect essays. Although they may use their notes and sources, they must work alone. Students will be allowed to look back at the answers they wrote to the short response questions, but they are not allowed to make changes to those answers. Have students read the directions for the essay and answer any task-related questions they may have. Students should be given paper on which to write their cause-and-effect essays.

2. **Initiate the Writing Task** If you are timing this part of the task, you may wish to suggest approximate times for students to begin writing and revising. If students wish to continue writing rather than revising, allow them to do so. Alert students when 5 minutes remain.

3. **Scoring Information** Use the scoring rubric on the next page to evaluate students' cause-and-effect essays.

4. **Essay Prompt** Write a cause-and-effect essay that describes causes of loneliness or unhappiness of the characters and the results, or effects, those feelings produce. Use details from all three texts to explain how and why these characters change. Give reasons why some people seem to adapt better, or faster, to problems than others do.

4-point Informative/Explanatory Writing Rubric					
Score	**Focus**	**Organization**	**Development of Evidence**	**Language and Vocabulary**	**Conventions**
4	The cause-and-effect essay is clearly stated, and the focus is strongly maintained.	The cause-and-effect essay has a clear and effective structure creating unity and completeness.	The cause-and-effect essay provides convincing support, including facts and details.	The cause-and-effect essay clearly and effectively expresses ideas, using precise language.	The cause-and-effect essay demonstrates a strong command of conventions.
3	The cause-and-effect essay is clear and maintained, though some loosely related material may be present.	The cause-and-effect essay has a clear structure, though there may be minor flaws and some ideas may be loosely connected.	The cause-and-effect essay provides adequate support that includes facts and details.	The cause-and-effect essay adequately expresses ideas, using precise and more general language.	The cause-and-effect essay demonstrates an adequate command of conventions.
2	The cause-and-effect essay is somewhat clear with some extraneous material or a minor drift in focus.	The cause-and-effect essay has an inconsistent structure, and flaws are evident.	The cause-and-effect essay provides cursory support that includes partial or uneven use of facts and details.	The cause-and-effect essay expresses ideas unevenly, using simplistic language.	The cause-and-effect essay demonstrates a partial command of conventions.
1	The cause-and-effect essay may be confusing, unfocused, or not sufficiently sustained.	The cause-and-effect essay has little or no discernible structure.	The cause-and-effect essay provides minimal support that includes little or no use of facts and details.	The cause-and-effect essay's expression of ideas is vague, lacks clarity, or is confusing.	The cause-and-effect essay demonstrates a lack of command of conventions.
0	A cause-and-effect essay gets no credit if it provides no evidence of the ability to compose a coherent explanation of causes and effects based on information from the sources.				

Ⓒ Common Core State Standards

Writing 2. Write informative/explanatory texts to examine a topic and convey ideas and information clearly. **Writing 9.** Draw evidence from literary or informational texts to support analysis, reflection, and research. **(Also Writing 2.a., Writing 2.b., Writing 2.c., Writing 10.)**

Cause for Change
Writing Task – Cause-and-Effect Essay

Student Directions:

Your Assignment Now you will review your notes and sources, and plan, draft, and revise your cause-and-effect essay. While you may use your notes and refer to the sources, you must work on your own. You may also refer to the answers you wrote to earlier questions, but you cannot change those answers.

Cause-and-Effect Essay Prompt Write a cause-and-effect essay that describes causes of loneliness or unhappiness of the characters and the results, or effects, those feelings produce. Use details from all three texts to explain how and why these characters change. Give reasons why some people seem to adapt better, or faster, than others do.

Scoring Information Your cause-and-effect essay will be assigned a score for

1. **Focus** – how clearly you focus on and explain the relationship between causes and effects

2. **Organization** – how well your essay groups related ideas together and includes transitions to connect ideas

3. **Elaboration** – how effectively you develop the topic with facts, details, and other information from sources

4. **Language and Vocabulary** – how well you use precise language and appropriate vocabulary to convey ideas and information

5. **Conventions** – how well you follow the rules of grammar, usage, capitalization, punctuation, and spelling

Now begin work on your cause-and-effect essay. Try to manage your time carefully so that you can

- plan your cause-and-effect essay
- write your cause-and-effect essay
- revise and edit for a final draft

Cause for Change: Writing Task – Cause-and-Effect Essay

Teacher Directions:

1. Publish Explain to students that publishing their writing is the last step in the writing process. Encourage students to use technology to publish and share their work, such as in an online collection, blog post, or e-mail.

2. Present Students will now have the option to present their cause-and-effect essays. Have students read and discuss their cause-and-effect essays in small groups. Use the list below to offer students some tips on listening and speaking.

While Listening to a Classmate...

- Keep purpose in mind and listen for causes and effects.
- Take notes on key ideas and questions you would like to ask.

While Speaking to Classmates...

- Make eye contact as much as possible.
- Speak clearly and at an appropriate pace.

Things to Do Together...

- Ask and respond to specific questions with details.
- Agree upon rules for conducting discussion. Listen to one another attentively, and do not interrupt the person who is speaking.
- Stick to the topic and elaborate on what others have said.

Ⓒ Common Core State Standards

Writing 6. With some guidance and support from adults, use technology, including the Internet, to produce and publish writing as well as to interact and collaborate with others; demonstrate sufficient command of keyboarding skills to type a minimum of two pages in a single sitting. **Speaking/ Listening 1.b.** Follow agreed-upon rules for discussions and carry out assigned roles. **Speaking/Listening 1.c.** Pose and respond to specific questions by making comments that contribute to the discussion and elaborate on the remarks of others. **Speaking/Listening 4.** Report on a topic or text, or present an opinion, sequencing ideas logically and using appropriate facts and relevant, descriptive details to support main ideas or themes; speak clearly at an appropriate pace. **Speaking/Listening 6.** Adapt speech to a variety of contexts and tasks, using formal English when appropriate to the task and situation.

Unit 5 Adventurers

Writing Focus: Argument

Write Like a Reporter

Argumentative Paragraph

Student Prompt Reread the story sections on p. 176 and pp. 183–187. Make a list of the boys' plans and their outcomes. Then write an argumentative paragraph that states your opinion about whether the skunk ladder plot had a better or worse outcome than the boys' other adventures. Use concrete details from the text to support your opinion. Include linking words, such as *consequently* and *specifically*, to make connections between your opinion and your evidence.

_____

_____

_____

_____

_____

_____

_____

_____

_____

_____

_____

_____

_____

_____

_____

_____

Write Like a Reporter
Argumentative Paragraph

Student Prompt, p. 134 Reread the story sections on p. 176 and pp. 183–187. Make a list of the boys' plans and their outcomes. Then write an argumentative paragraph that states your opinion about whether the skunk ladder plot had a better or worse outcome than the boys' other adventures. Use concrete details from the text to support your opinion. Include linking words, such as *consequently* and *specifically*, to make connections between your opinion and your evidence.

Writing to Sources As students reread the story, have them make a list of all the boys' adventures and make notes on how the boys' plans turn out. Ask students to consider how the skunk ladder plot compares with the boys' other adventures. Remind students to reread the text carefully and find clear evidence from the text that supports their opinions. Also remind them to use linking words and phrases to logically organize their opinions and supporting evidence.

Students' paragraphs should:

- clearly state an opinion regarding the events of the text
- support the opinion with relevant evidence
- use linking words that clarify the relationship between the opinion and evidence
- demonstrate strong command of the conventions of standard written English

---

© **Common Core State Standards**

Writing 1. Write opinion pieces on topics or texts, supporting a point of view with reasons and information. **Writing 9.a.** Apply grade 5 Reading standards to literature (e.g., "Compare and contrast two or more characters, settings, or events in a story or a drama, drawing on specific details in the text [e.g., how characters interact]").

Connect the Texts
Argumentative Essay

Student Prompt Look back at *The Skunk Ladder* and "Books and Adventure," paying attention to the boys' friendships and the things they do together. Which detail or event best explains why these boys have such strong friendships? Write a short argumentative essay that states your opinion. Support your reasons with facts and details from both texts. Include a concluding statement that summarizes your opinion.

_____

_____

_____

_____

_____

_____

_____

_____

_____

_____

_____

_____

_____

_____

_____

_____

Connect the Texts
Argumentative Essay

Student Prompt, p. 136 Look back at *The Skunk Ladder* and "Books and Adventure," paying attention to the boys' friendships and the things they do together. Which detail or event best explains why these boys have such strong friendships? Write a short argumentative essay that states your opinion. Support your reasons with facts and details from both texts. Include a concluding statement that summarizes your opinion.

Writing to Sources After students reread the texts, discuss their opinions about how the boys' friendships are portrayed in each text. Ask them which detail or event best represents the boys' friendships. Have them support their reasons with specific facts and details drawn from both texts. Ask them to include a concluding statement that sums up their opinions.

		4-point Argument Writing Rubric			
Score	**Statement of Purpose/Focus**	**Organization**	**Development of Evidence**	**Language and Vocabulary**	**Conventions**
4	Opinion is clearly conveyed and well supported; response is focused.	Organization is clear and effective, creating a sense of cohesion.	Evidence is thorough and persuasive, and includes facts and details.	Ideas are clearly and effectively conveyed, using precise language and/or domain-specific vocabulary.	Command of conventions is strongly demonstrated.
3	Opinion is clear, adequately supported; response is generally focused.	Organization is clear, though minor flaws may be present and some ideas may be disconnected.	Evidence is adequate and includes facts and details.	Ideas are adequately conveyed, using both precise and more general language; may include domain-specific vocabulary.	Command of conventions is sufficiently demonstrated.
2	Opinion is somewhat supported; response may lack focus or include unnecessary material.	Organization is inconsistent, and flaws are apparent.	Evidence is uneven or incomplete; insufficient use of facts and details.	Ideas are unevenly conveyed, using overly-simplistic language; lack of domain-specific vocabulary.	Command of conventions is uneven.
1	The response may be confusing, unfocused; opinion not sufficiently supported.	Organization is poor or nonexistent.	Evidence is poor or nonexistent.	Ideas are conveyed in a vague, unclear, or confusing manner.	There is very little command of conventions.
0	The response shows no evidence of the ability to construct a coherent opinion essay using information from sources.				

ⓒ **Common Core State Standards**

Writing 1. Write opinion pieces on topics or texts, supporting a point of view with reasons and information. **Writing 9.a.** Apply grade 5 Reading standards to literature (e.g., "Compare and contrast two or more characters, settings, or events in a story or a drama, drawing on specific details in the text [e.g., how characters interact]"). **Writing 9.b.** Apply grade 5 Reading standards to informational texts (e.g., "Explain how an author uses reasons and evidence to support particular points in a text, identifying which reasons and evidence support which point[s]").

Write Like a Reporter
Argumentative Paragraph

Student Prompt Reread the description of the ship's remains on pp. 210–215. Take notes on the text's details and review the photographs. In your opinion, which artifact best highlights the tragedy of the wreck? Write an argumentative paragraph that states the reasons for your opinion. Include accurate quotations and facts to support your opinion. Also include persuasive words and phrases, such as *therefore* and *most importantly*, to link and clarify your opinion to your reasons.

_____

_____

_____

_____

_____

_____

_____

_____

_____

_____

_____

_____

_____

_____

_____

Write Like a Reporter
Argumentative Paragraph

Student Prompt, p. 138 Reread the description of the ship's remains on pp. 210–215. Take notes on the text's details and review the photographs. In your opinion, which artifact best highlights the tragedy of the wreck? Write an argumentative paragraph that states the reasons for your opinion. Include accurate quotations and facts to support your opinion. Also include persuasive words and phrases, such as *therefore* and *most importantly*, to link and clarify your opinion to your reasons.

Writing to Sources As students reread the expository text, have them pay attention to the photographs and descriptive details. Ask them which details are the most effective and have them explain their opinions. Remind students to reread carefully and find clear evidence from the text that supports their claims. Students' responses should include accurate quotations and detailed descriptions of their chosen images.

Students' paragraphs should:

- clearly state an opinion regarding the ship's artifacts
- support the opinion with relevant evidence and concrete details
- use linking words that clarify the relationship between the opinion and reasons
- demonstrate strong command of the conventions of standard written English

© **Common Core State Standards**

Writing 1. Write opinion pieces on topics or texts, supporting a point of view with reasons and information. **Writing 9.b.** Apply grade 5 Reading standards to informational texts (e.g., "Explain how an author uses reasons and evidence to support particular points in a text, identifying which reasons and evidence support which point[s]").

Connect the Texts
Argumentative Essay

Student Prompt Reread *The Unsinkable Wreck of the R.M.S* Titanic and "Shipwreck Season." Based on the details in each text, do you agree with Daniel's opinion that "it was no small thing to be a surfman"? Write a short essay that states your opinion. Carefully reread both texts to find evidence that supports your claim. Remember to include specific facts, accurate quotations, and concrete details from both texts.

_____

_____

_____

_____

_____

_____

_____

_____

_____

_____

_____

_____

_____

_____

_____

_____

_____

_____

Connect the Texts
Argumentative Essay

Student Prompt, p. 140 Reread *The Unsinkable Wreck of the R.M.S* Titanic and "Shipwreck Season." Based on the details in each text, do you agree with Daniel's opinion that "it was no small thing to be a surfman"? Write a short essay that states your opinion. Carefully reread both texts to find evidence that supports your claim. Remember to include specific facts, accurate quotations, and concrete details from both texts.

Writing to Sources Discuss students' opinions about shipwrecks and rescue teams. Ask them why they agree or disagree with Daniel's conclusion about being a surfman. Then have them carefully reread both texts to find specific evidence, such as facts, details, and quotations, to support their claims. Remind them to support their opinions with details from both texts.

	4-point Argument Writing Rubric				
Score	Statement of Purpose/Focus	Organization	Development of Evidence	Language and Vocabulary	Conventions
4	Opinion is clearly conveyed and well supported; response is focused.	Organization is clear and effective, creating a sense of cohesion.	Evidence is thorough and persuasive, and includes facts and details.	Ideas are clearly and effectively conveyed, using precise language and/or domain-specific vocabulary.	Command of conventions is strongly demonstrated.
3	Opinion is clear, adequately supported; response is generally focused.	Organization is clear, though minor flaws may be present and some ideas may be disconnected.	Evidence is adequate and includes facts and details.	Ideas are adequately conveyed, using both precise and more general language; may include domain-specific vocabulary.	Command of conventions is sufficiently demonstrated.
2	Opinion is somewhat supported; response may lack focus or include unnecessary material.	Organization is inconsistent, and flaws are apparent.	Evidence is uneven or incomplete; insufficient use of facts and details.	Ideas are unevenly conveyed, using overly-simplistic language; lack of domain-specific vocabulary.	Command of conventions is uneven.
1	The response may be confusing, unfocused; opinion not sufficiently supported.	Organization is poor or nonexistent.	Evidence is poor or nonexistent.	Ideas are conveyed in a vague, unclear, or confusing manner.	There is very little command of conventions.
0	The response shows no evidence of the ability to construct a coherent opinion essay using information from sources.				

Ⓒ **Common Core State Standards**

Writing 1. Write opinion pieces on topics or texts, supporting a point of view with reasons and information. **Writing 9.a.** Apply grade 5 Reading standards to literature (e.g., "Compare and contrast two or more characters, settings, or events in a story or a drama, drawing on specific details in the text [e.g., how characters interact]"). **Writing 9.b.** Apply grade 5 Reading standards to informational texts (e.g., "Explain how an author uses reasons and evidence to support particular points in a text, identifying which reasons and evidence support which point[s]").

Write Like a Reporter
Argumentative Paragraph

Student Prompt Reread the interview on pp. 238–244 and make a list of the details Ellen Ochoa gives about training and working in space. Which part of being an astronaut seems the hardest? To support your opinion, write a persuasive paragraph that includes Ochoa's details. Support your reasons with relevant evidence and concrete details, such as accurate quotations from the interview. Include linking words, such as *consequently* and *specifically*, to clarify the reasons for your opinion.

_____

_____

_____

_____

_____

_____

_____

_____

_____

_____

_____

_____

_____

_____

_____

_____

_____

Write Like a Reporter
Argumentative Paragraph

Student Prompt, p. 142 Reread the interview on pp. 238–244 and make a list of the details Ellen Ochoa gives about training and working in space. Which part of being an astronaut seems the hardest? To support your opinion, write a persuasive paragraph that includes Ochoa's details. Support your reasons with relevant evidence and concrete details, such as accurate quotations from the interview. Include linking words, such as *consequently* and *specifically*, to clarify the reasons for your opinion.

Writing to Sources After students reread the interview, ask them to list the details Ellen Ochoa gives about training and working in space. Have them analyze these details to determine which part of being an astronaut is hardest and why. Remind students to reread carefully and find concrete details and quotations to support their opinions. Students' responses should include linking words that draw connections between their opinions and evidence. Remind students to quote accurately as they write.

Students' paragraphs should:

- clearly state an opinion regarding the challenges of being an astronaut
- support the opinion with relevant evidence and concrete details
- use linking words that clarify the relationship between the opinion and reasons
- demonstrate strong command of the conventions of standard written English

---

Ⓒ **Common Core State Standards**

Writing 1. Write opinion pieces on topics or texts, supporting a point of view with reasons and information. **Writing 9.b.** Apply grade 5 Reading standards to informational texts (e.g., "Explain how an author uses reasons and evidence to support particular points in a text, identifying which reasons and evidence support which point[s]").

Connect the Texts
Argumentative Essay

> **Student Prompt** Look back at *Talk with an Astronaut* and "Women Astronauts" and pay attention to how each woman became an astronaut. Which do you think contributed more to each astronaut's success: her educational background or a positive attitude? Write a short essay that states your opinion. Carefully reread both texts to find evidence that supports your claim. Remember to include specific facts, accurate quotations, and concrete details from both texts.

_____

_____

_____

_____

_____

_____

_____

_____

_____

_____

_____

_____

_____

_____

Connect the Texts
Argumentative Essay

> **Student Prompt, p. 144** Look back at *Talk with an Astronaut* and "Women Astronauts" and pay attention to how each woman became an astronaut. Which do you think contributed more to each astronaut's success: her educational background or a positive attitude? Write a short essay that states your opinion. Carefully reread both texts to find evidence that supports your claim. Remember to include specific facts, accurate quotations, and concrete details from both texts.

Writing to Sources After students reread both texts, discuss their opinions about the astronauts' educational training and positive attitudes. Have them consider the cause-and-effect relationships between education and success and between attitude and success. As students write, remind them to base their opinions on evidence from both texts, including specific facts, accurate quotations, and concrete details.

Score	Statement of Purpose/Focus	Organization	Development of Evidence	Language and Vocabulary	Conventions
4	Opinion is clearly conveyed and well supported; response is focused.	Organization is clear and effective, creating a sense of cohesion.	Evidence is thorough and persuasive, and includes facts and details.	Ideas are clearly and effectively conveyed, using precise language and/or domain-specific vocabulary.	Command of conventions is strongly demonstrated.
3	Opinion is clear, adequately supported; response is generally focused.	Organization is clear, though minor flaws may be present and some ideas may be disconnected.	Evidence is adequate and includes facts and details.	Ideas are adequately conveyed, using both precise and more general language; may include domain-specific vocabulary.	Command of conventions is sufficiently demonstrated.
2	Opinion is somewhat supported; response may lack focus or include unnecessary material.	Organization is inconsistent, and flaws are apparent.	Evidence is uneven or incomplete; insufficient use of facts and details.	Ideas are unevenly conveyed, using overly-simplistic language; lack of domain-specific vocabulary.	Command of conventions is uneven.
1	The response may be confusing, unfocused; opinion not sufficiently supported.	Organization is poor or nonexistent.	Evidence is poor or nonexistent.	Ideas are conveyed in a vague, unclear, or confusing manner.	There is very little command of conventions.
0	The response shows no evidence of the ability to construct a coherent opinion essay using information from sources.				

4-point Argument Writing Rubric

© **Common Core State Standards**

Writing 1. Write opinion pieces on topics or texts, supporting a point of view with reasons and information. **Writing 9.b.** Apply grade 5 Reading standards to informational texts (e.g., "Explain how an author uses reasons and evidence to support particular points in a text, identifying which reasons and evidence support which point[s]").

Write Like a Reporter
Argumentative Paragraph

Student Prompt Reread the descriptions of the creatures on pp. 269–273. Compare and contrast the text descriptions with the illustrations. How do the illustrations add to the meaning and tone of the text? Are they more effective or less effective than the text details? Write a paragraph that states your opinion. Support your opinion with relevant evidence, concrete details, and accurate quotations. Conclude with a sentence that summarizes your opinion in a convincing way.

_____

_____

_____

_____

_____

_____

_____

_____

_____

_____

_____

_____

_____

_____

Write Like a Reporter
Argumentative Paragraph

Student Prompt, p. 146 Reread the descriptions of the creatures on pp. 269–273. Compare and contrast the text descriptions with the illustrations. How do the illustrations add to the meaning and tone of the text? Are they more effective or less effective than the text details? Write a paragraph that states your opinion. Support your opinion with relevant evidence, concrete details, and accurate quotations. Conclude with a sentence that summarizes your opinion in a convincing way.

Writing to Sources After students reread, ask them to identify the details the author uses to describe the giant reptiles. Have them compare and contrast these details with the accompanying illustrations and ask which are more effective: the text descriptions or illustrations. Before students write, remind them to support their opinions with relevant evidence and concrete details. Also remind them to conclude their paragraph with a convincing final sentence that sums up their opinion.

Students' paragraphs should:

- clearly state an opinion regarding the effectiveness of the illustrations or text descriptions
- support the opinion with relevant evidence and concrete details
- provide a concluding statement that summarizes their argument
- demonstrate strong command of the conventions of standard written English

© Common Core State Standards

Writing 1. Write opinion pieces on topics or texts, supporting a point of view with reasons and information. **Writing 9.a.** Apply grade 5 Reading standards to literature (e.g., "Compare and contrast two or more characters, settings, or events in a story or a drama, drawing on specific details in the text [e.g., how characters interact]").

Name _____

Connect the Texts
Argumentative Essay

Student Prompt Reread *Journey to the Center of the Earth* and "The Sea Battle."
Compare and contrast both versions of the story. Do you think the drama accurately
represents the events and character interactions from the novel? Write a short essay that
states your opinion. Reread both texts carefully and find evidence that supports your
claim. Remember to include accurate quotations and concrete details from both texts.

_____

_____

_____

_____

_____

_____

_____

_____

_____

_____

_____

_____

_____

_____

_____

_____

_____

Connect the Texts
Argumentative Essay

Student Prompt, p. 148 Reread *Journey to the Center of the Earth* and "The Sea Battle." Compare and contrast both versions of the story. Do you think the drama accurately represents the events and character interactions from the novel? Write a short essay that states your opinion. Reread both texts carefully and find evidence that supports your claim. Remember to include accurate quotations and concrete details from both texts.

Writing to Sources Before students reread, remind them that "The Sea Battle" is an adaptation of *Journey to the Center of the Earth*. After they read, have them compare and contrast the two accounts. Ask them whether the drama is an accurate adaptation of the novel. Have them consider the way the events and characters' interactions are portrayed. Remind students to include quotations and details from both texts.

	4-point Argument Writing Rubric				
Score	**Statement of Purpose/Focus**	**Organization**	**Development of Evidence**	**Language and Vocabulary**	**Conventions**
4	Opinion is clearly conveyed and well supported; response is focused.	Organization is clear and effective, creating a sense of cohesion.	Evidence is thorough and persuasive, and includes facts and details.	Ideas are clearly and effectively conveyed, using precise language and/or domain-specific vocabulary.	Command of conventions is strongly demonstrated.
3	Opinion is clear, adequately supported; response is generally focused.	Organization is clear, though minor flaws may be present and some ideas may be disconnected.	Evidence is adequate and includes facts and details.	Ideas are adequately conveyed, using both precise and more general language; may include domain-specific vocabulary.	Command of conventions is sufficiently demonstrated.
2	Opinion is somewhat supported; response may lack focus or include unnecessary material.	Organization is inconsistent, and flaws are apparent.	Evidence is uneven or incomplete; insufficient use of facts and details.	Ideas are unevenly conveyed, using overly-simplistic language; lack of domain-specific vocabulary.	Command of conventions is uneven.
1	The response may be confusing, unfocused; opinion not sufficiently supported.	Organization is poor or nonexistent.	Evidence is poor or nonexistent.	Ideas are conveyed in a vague, unclear, or confusing manner.	There is very little command of conventions.
0	The response shows no evidence of the ability to construct a coherent opinion essay using information from sources.				

Ⓒ Common Core State Standards

Writing 1. Write opinion pieces on topics or texts, supporting a point of view with reasons and information. **Writing 9.a.** Apply grade 5 Reading standards to literature (e.g., "Compare and contrast two or more characters, settings, or events in a story or a drama, drawing on specific details in the text [e.g., how characters interact]").

Write Like a Reporter
Argumentative Paragraph

Student Prompt Reread the nonfiction account *Ghost Towns of the American West.* Then make a list of events, facts, and details in sequence. Which event or detail most contributed to the creation of ghost towns in the West? Write a paragraph that states your opinion. Use relevant evidence and concrete details from the text as support. Use linking phrases, such as *for instance*, *in order to*, and *in addition*, to make your reasoning clear.

_____

_____

_____

_____

_____

_____

_____

_____

_____

_____

_____

_____

_____

_____

_____

_____

Write Like a Reporter
Argumentative Paragraph

> **Student Prompt, p. 150**. Reread the nonfiction account *Ghost Towns of the American West*. Then make a list of events, facts, and details in sequence. Which event or detail most contributed to the creation of ghost towns in the West? Write a paragraph that states your opinion. Use relevant evidence and concrete details from the text as support. Use linking phrases, such as *for instance*, *in order to*, and *in addition*, to make your reasoning clear.

Writing to Sources After students reread, ask them to identify the details and events the author includes to explain how ghost towns were made in the American West. Have them compare and contrast these details to determine which was the most influential. Before students write, remind them to support their opinions with relevant evidence and concrete details. Also remind them to use linking transitions to clarify their line of reasoning.

Students' paragraphs should:

- clearly state an opinion regarding the creation of ghost towns in the West
- support the opinion with relevant evidence and concrete details
- use linking phrases to clarify a line of reasoning
- demonstrate strong command of the conventions of standard written English

---

Ⓒ **Common Core State Standards**

Writing 1. Write opinion pieces on topics or texts, supporting a point of view with reasons and information. **Writing 9.b.** Apply grade 5 Reading standards to informational texts (e.g., "Explain how an author uses reasons and evidence to support particular points in a text, identifying which reasons and evidence support which point[s]").

Connect the Texts
Argumentative Essay

> **Student Prompt** Look back at *Ghost Towns of the American West* and "Gold Dreams."
> Compare and contrast both portrayals of the American gold rush. Do you think John made
> the right decision to stay in Goldfield? Using concrete details from the nonfiction account,
> write a short persuasive essay that states your opinion about John. Reread both texts
> carefully and find evidence that supports your opinion. Remember to include accurate
> quotations and concrete details from both texts.

_____

_____

_____

_____

_____

_____

_____

_____

_____

_____

_____

_____

_____

_____

_____

_____

Connect the Texts

Argumentative Persuasive Essay

Student Prompt, p. 152 Look back at *Ghost Towns of the American West* and "Gold Dreams." Compare and contrast both portrayals of the American gold rush. Do you think John made the right decision to stay in Goldfield? Using concrete details from the nonfiction account, write a short persuasive essay that states your opinion about John. Reread both texts carefully and find evidence that supports your opinion. Remember to include accurate quotations and concrete details from both texts.

Writing to Sources Remind students that *Ghost Towns of the American West* is a nonfiction account and that "Gold Dreams" is a work of historical fiction. After students reread, have them compare and contrast both portrayals of the American gold rush. Ask them to use concrete details from the nonfiction account to decide whether the fictional character John made the right decision to become a gold miner. Remind students to include quotations and details from both texts.

4-point Argument Writing Rubric					
Score	Statement of Purpose/Focus	Organization	Development of Evidence	Language and Vocabulary	Conventions
4	Opinion is clearly conveyed and well supported; response is focused.	Organization is clear and effective, creating a sense of cohesion.	Evidence is thorough and persuasive, and includes facts and details.	Ideas are clearly and effectively conveyed, using precise language and/or domain-specific vocabulary.	Command of conventions is strongly demonstrated.
3	Opinion is clear, adequately supported; response is generally focused.	Organization is clear, though minor flaws may be present and some ideas may be disconnected.	Evidence is adequate and includes facts and details.	Ideas are adequately conveyed, using both precise and more general language; may include domain-specific vocabulary.	Command of conventions is sufficiently demonstrated.
2	Opinion is somewhat supported; response may lack focus or include unnecessary material.	Organization is inconsistent, and flaws are apparent.	Evidence is uneven or incomplete; insufficient use of facts and details.	Ideas are unevenly conveyed, using overly-simplistic language; lack of domain-specific vocabulary.	Command of conventions is uneven.
1	The response may be confusing, unfocused; opinion not sufficiently supported.	Organization is poor or nonexistent.	Evidence is poor or nonexistent.	Ideas are conveyed in a vague, unclear, or confusing manner.	There is very little command of conventions.
0	The response shows no evidence of the ability to construct a coherent opinion essay using information from sources.				

© Common Core State Standards

Writing 1. Write opinion pieces on topics or texts, supporting a point of view with reasons and information. **Writing 9.a.** Apply grade 5 Reading standards to literature (e.g., "Compare and contrast two or more characters, settings, or events in a story or a drama, drawing on specific details in the text [e.g., how characters interact]"). **Writing 9.b.** Apply grade 5 Reading standards to informational texts (e.g., "Explain how an author uses reasons and evidence to support particular points in a text, identifying which reasons and evidence support which point[s]").

Prove It!
Argumentative Essay

Adventure Seekers

Argumentative Essay

In this unit, students have read examples of persuasive writing and have had the opportunity to write in this mode. Remind students of texts and writing tasks (such as Write Like a Reporter and Connect the Texts) in which they have encountered and practiced argumentative writing.

Key Features of an Argumentative Essay

- states an opinion, or a claim, on a topic
- includes reasons and relevant evidence, such as facts and details, to support the claim
- organizes reasons and evidence in a clear and logical order
- includes transition words, phrases, and clauses to link reasons to the opinion
- has an introduction, body, and conclusion

Writing Task Overview

Each unit writing task provides students with an opportunity to write to sources. To successfully complete the task, students must analyze, synthesize, and evaluate multiple complex texts and create their own written response.

Adventure Seekers

Part 1: Students will reread and take notes on the selected sources. They will then respond to several questions about these sources and discuss their written responses with partners or in small groups.

Part 2: Students will work individually to plan, write, and revise their own argumentative essay.

Scorable Products: short responses, argumentative essay

Adventure Seekers: Writing Task – Short Response

Teacher Directions:

1. Introduce the Sources Refer students to the following texts in the Student Edition:

1. *The Skunk Ladder,* pp. 174–187

2. *Talk with an Astronaut,* pp. 234–245

3. *Ghost Towns of the American West,* pp. 290–301

Explain to students that they will need to draw evidence and support from the texts above in order to answer evidence-based short response questions and to write an argumentative essay. Students should take notes and categorize information as they closely reread the texts. Students should be given paper or a relevant graphic organizer from the TR DVD for note-taking.

2. Provide Student Directions and Scoring Information (p. 158) Answer any task-related questions students may have. If necessary, provide additional paper for students to write their responses.

3. Initiate the Writing Task If you are timing this part of the task, you may wish to alert students when half the allotted time has elapsed and again when 5 minutes remain.

4. Facilitate Collaboration After students have completed their written responses to the evidence-based short response questions, assign partners or small groups and have them discuss their responses. If students struggle to work together productively, provide them with tips and strategies for expressing their ideas and building on others'.

© **Common Core State Standards**

Writing 1. Write opinion pieces on topics or texts, supporting a point of view with reasons and information. **Speaking/Listening 1.** Engage effectively in a range of collaborative discussions (one-on-one, in groups, and teacher-led) with diverse partners on grade 5 topics and texts, building on others' ideas and expressing their own clearly. **(Also Writing 1.a., Writing 1.b., Writing 1.c., Writing 1.d.)**

Scoring Information

Use the following 2-point scoring rubrics to evaluate students' answers to the evidence-based short response questions.

1. Find details in the three selections that tell what the adventurers do and think. How are the adventurers different? How are they alike? Use the text details in your answer.

	Analysis Rubric
2	The response: • demonstrates the ability to analyze similarities and differences between the adventurers • includes specific details that make reference to the texts
1	The response: • demonstrates a limited ability to analyze similarities and differences between the adventurers • includes some details that make reference to the texts
0	A response receives no credit if it demonstrates no ability to analyze similarities and differences between the adventurers or includes no relevant details from the texts.

2. Think about the traits you identified in the first question. In your opinion, which three traits are *most important* for all or almost all adventurers? Make a generalization. Include a detail from each text that helped form your opinion.

	Synthesis Rubric
2	The response: • demonstrates the ability to synthesize information from the sources in order to make a generalization • includes specific details that make reference to the texts
1	The response: • demonstrates a limited ability to synthesize information from the sources in order to make a generalization • includes some details that make reference to the texts
0	A response receives no credit if it demonstrates no ability to synthesize information from the sources or includes no relevant details from the texts.

3. Arguments must be logical. Evaluate your generalization, or judge whether it is valid, by providing evidence of how Eddie, Ellen Ochoa, and the Western settlers all show those traits in some way. Then rank the traits in order of importance.

	Evaluation Rubric	
2	The response: • demonstrates the ability to evaluate a generalization and rank traits • includes specific details that make reference to the texts	
1	The response: • demonstrates a limited ability to evaluate a generalization and rank traits • includes some details that make reference to the texts	
0	A response receives no credit if it demonstrates no ability to evaluate a generalization or includes no relevant details from the texts.	

© **Common Core State Standards**

Writing 8. Recall relevant information from experiences or gather relevant information from print and digital sources; summarize or paraphrase information in notes and finished work, and provide a list of sources. **Writing 9.** Draw evidence from literary or informational texts to support analysis, reflection, and research.

Adventure Seekers
Writing Task – Short Response

Student Directions:

Your Assignment You will reread several selections from Unit 5 and take notes on these sources. Then you will answer three questions about these materials. You may refer to your notes or to any of the sources as often as you like.

Sources

1. *The Skunk Ladder,* pp. 174–187

2. *Talk with an Astronaut,* pp. 234–245

3. *Ghost Towns of the American West,* pp. 290–301

Be sure to read closely and take good notes. Your sources and notes will be the basis for writing your own argumentative essay in the second half of this writing task.

Evidence-Based Short Response Questions Answer the short response questions on the lines provided below each question. Your answers to these questions will be scored. Be sure to base your answers on the sources you have just read. Remember that you may refer back to your notes or to any of the sources.

After you have answered the questions, you will discuss your responses with a partner. Your teacher will let you know when to begin the discussion part of this task.

Scoring Information Your responses will be scored based on how you demonstrate the ability to:

- compare information across texts
- include relevant evidence from the sources as support
- identify, analyze, synthesize, and evaluate information from the sources
- distinguish key evidence and support from irrelevant information

Evidence-Based Short Response Questions

1. Find details in the three selections that tell what the adventurers do and think. How are the adventurers different? How are they alike? Use the text details in your answer.

_____

_____

_____

_____

2. Think about the traits you identified in the first question. In your opinion, which three traits are *most important* for all or almost all adventurers? Make a generalization. Include a detail from each text that helped form your opinion.

_____

_____

_____

_____

3. Arguments must be logical. Evaluate your generalization, or judge whether it is valid, by providing evidence of how Eddie, Ellen Ochoa, and the Western settlers all show those traits in some way. Then rank the traits in order of importance.

_____

_____

_____

_____

Collaborative Discussion

After you have written your responses to the questions, discuss your ideas. Your teacher will assign you a partner or small group and let you know when to begin.

Adventure Seekers: Writing Task – Argumentative Essay

Teacher Directions:

1. **Provide Student Directions and Scoring Information (p. 162)** Explain to students that they will now review their notes and sources, and plan, draft, and revise their argumentative essays. Although they may use their notes and sources, they must work alone. Students will be allowed to look back at the answers they wrote to the short response questions, but they will not be allowed to make changes to those answers. Have students read the directions for the argumentative essay, and answer any task-related questions they may have. Students should be given paper on which to write their argumentative essays.

2. **Initiate the Writing Task** If you are timing this part of the task, you may wish to suggest approximate times for students to begin writing and revising. If students wish to continue writing rather than revising, allow them to do so. Alert students when 5 minutes remain.

3. **Scoring Information** Use the scoring rubric on the next page to evaluate students' argumentative essays.

4. **Essay Prompt** Use what you have learned from reading *The Skunk Ladder, Talk with an Astronaut,* and *Ghost Towns of the American West* to write an argumentative essay that states your opinion on the three most important, or key, traits of adventure seekers. Give at least one reason why an adventurer must have each trait. Use examples from the selections to explain and support your reasons. Be sure to follow the conventions of written English.

4-point Argument Writing Rubric					
Score	**Statement of Purpose/Focus**	**Organization**	**Development of Evidence**	**Language and Vocabulary**	**Conventions**
4	Opinion is clearly conveyed and well supported; argument is focused.	Organization is clear and effective, creating a sense of cohesion.	Evidence is thorough and persuasive, and includes facts and details.	Ideas are clearly and effectively conveyed, using precise language and/or domain-specific vocabulary.	Command of conventions is strongly demonstrated.
3	Opinion is clear, adequately supported; argument is generally focused.	Organization is clear, though minor flaws may be present and some ideas may be disconnected.	Evidence is adequate and includes facts and details	Ideas are adequately conveyed, using both precise and more general language; may include domain-specific vocabulary.	Command of conventions is sufficiently demonstrated.
2	Opinion is somewhat supported; lacks focus or includes unnecessary material.	Organization is inconsistent, and flaws are apparent.	Evidence is uneven or incomplete; insufficient use of facts and details.	Ideas are unevenly conveyed, using overly simplistic language; lacks domain-specific vocabulary.	Command of conventions is uneven.
1	Argument may be confusing, unfocused; opinion is not supported.	Organization is poor or nonexistent.	Evidence is poor or nonexistent.	Ideas are conveyed in a vague, unclear, or confusing manner.	There is very little command of conventions
0	The response shows no evidence of the ability to construct a coherent argumentative essay using information from sources.				

© **Common Core State Standards**

Writing 1. Write opinion pieces on topics or texts, supporting a point of view with reasons and information. **Writing 9.** Draw evidence from literary or informational texts to support analysis, reflection, and research. **(Also Writing 1.a., Writing 1.b., Writing 10.)**

Writing Task – Argumentative Essay

Student Directions:

Your Assignment Now you will review your notes and sources, and plan, draft, and revise your argumentative essay. While you may use your notes and refer to the sources, you must work on your own. You may also refer to the answers you wrote to earlier questions, but you cannot change those answers.

Argumentative Essay Prompt Use what you have learned from reading *The Skunk Ladder, Talk with an Astronaut,* and *Ghost Towns of the American West* to write an argumentative essay that states your opinion on the three most important, or key, traits of adventure seekers. Give at least one reason why an adventurer must have each trait. Use examples from the selections to explain and support your reasons. Be sure to follow the conventions of written English.

Scoring Information Your argumentative essay will be assigned a score for

1. **Focus** – how well you state your opinion on the topic and support it throughout the essay

2. **Organization** – how well you group ideas logically, use reasons to support your opinion, and include facts and details to support your reasons

3. **Elaboration** – how well you use words, phrases, and clauses to link your opinion and reasons

4. **Language and Vocabulary** – how well you express your ideas using concrete and appropriate language

5. **Conventions** – how well you follow the rules of grammar, usage, capitalization, punctuation, and spelling

Now begin work on your argumentative essay. Try to manage your time carefully so that you can:

- plan your argumentative essay
- write your argumentative essay
- revise and edit for a final draft

Adventure Seekers: Writing Task – Argumentative Essay

Teacher Directions:

1. Publish Explain to students that publishing their writing is the last step in the writing process. If time permits, have students review one another's essays and incorporate any comments their classmates have. Discuss different ways students might use technology to collaborate with others and to produce and publish writing.

2. Present Students will now have the option to present their arguments. Have students give presentations with four slides (or graphics): one for their opinion, and one stating each reason for their opinion. Use the list below to offer students some tips on listening and speaking.

While Listening to a Classmate...

- Sit upright and show interest.
- Take notes on what the speaker says.

While Speaking to Classmates...

- Stand upright and show interest.
- Point to, or otherwise engage with, each slide or graphic as you show it.
- Speak clearly and vary your tone of voice and pace to speak persuasively.

Things to Do Together...

- Follow agreed-upon rules for presentations and discussions afterward.
- Ask and answer questions to clarify information in the presentation.
- Comment on each other's ideas.

© Common Core State Standards

Writing 6. With some guidance and support from adults, use technology, including the Internet, to produce and publish writing as well as to interact and collaborate with others; demonstrate sufficient command of keyboarding skills to type a minimum of two pages in a single sitting. **Speaking/Listening 1.b.** Follow agreed-upon rules for discussions and carry out assigned roles. **Speaking/Listening 1.c.** Pose and respond to specific questions by making comments that contribute to the discussion and elaborate on the remarks of others. **Speaking/Listening 5.** Include multimedia components (e.g., graphics, sound) and visual displays in presentations when appropriate to enhance the development of main ideas or themes.

Unit 6 The Unexpected

Writing Focus: Narrative

Name _____

Write Like a Reporter
Narrative Paragraph

Student Prompt Reread the section on pp. 326–335 and retell the facts. Take notes on the details about bats, such as behavioral traits and eating habits. Then write a one-paragraph story from a bat's perspective. Establish the situation by explaining why some people might be afraid of bats. Then use description to develop a narrative of the bats' positive experience in Austin. Include transitional words and phrases to clarify the sequence of events.

_____

_____

_____

_____

_____

_____

_____

_____

_____

_____

_____

_____

_____

_____

_____

_____

_____

_____

Write Like a Reporter
Narrative Paragraph

Student Prompt, p. 166 Reread the section on pp. 326–335 and retell the facts. Take notes on the details about bats, such as behavioral traits and eating habits. Then write a one-paragraph story from a bat's perspective. Establish the situation by explaining why some people might be afraid of bats. Then use description to develop a narrative of the bats' positive experience in Austin. Include transitional words and phrases to clarify the sequence of events.

Writing to Sources As students reread, have them make a list of all the facts and details about bats they can find in the text. Ask them to imagine how this information would be different if it were told from the bats' perspective. Before students write, remind them that description is a narrative technique. Also remind them to use transitional words and phrases to clarify the sequence of events.

Students' paragraphs should:

- orient the reader by establishing the bats' situation
- use transitional words and phrases to clarify the sequence of events
- use narrative techniques, such as description, to develop the bats' experience
- demonstrate strong command of the conventions of standard written English

---

Ⓒ **Common Core State Standards**

Writing 3. Write narratives to develop real or imagined experiences or events using effective technique, descriptive details, and clear event sequences. **Writing 9.b.** Apply grade 5 Reading standards to informational texts (e.g., "Explain how an author uses reasons and evidence to support particular points in a text, identifying which reasons and evidence support which point[s]").

Connect the Texts
Narrative Journal Entry

Student Prompt Look back at *The Truth About Austin's Amazing Bats* and "The Animals in My Life." Consider Ron Fridell's reasons for writing about Austin's bats. Then write a two-paragraph journal entry from Ron Fridell's perspective that depicts his experience watching the bats in Austin. Reread both texts carefully to find sensory details to include in your narrative. Remember to organize your narrative so that events unfold naturally.

_____

_____

_____

_____

_____

_____

_____

_____

_____

_____

_____

_____

_____

_____

_____

_____

_____

Connect the Texts
Narrative Journal Entry

Student Prompt, p. 168 Look back at *The Truth About Austin's Amazing Bats* and "The Animals in My Life." Consider Ron Fridell's reasons for writing about Austin's bats. Then write a two-paragraph journal entry from Ron Fridell's perspective that depicts his experience watching the bats in Austin. Reread both texts carefully to find sensory details to include in your narrative. Remember to organize your narrative so that events unfold naturally.

Writing to Sources Remind students that *The Truth About Austin's Amazing Bats* and "The Animals in My Life" have the same author. After students reread, ask them to consider why Ron Fridell chose to write about bats. Have them use the sensory details Fridell gives to write a two-paragraph journal entry from his perspective. Remind them to organize their narratives so events unfold naturally.

4-point Narrative Writing Rubric					
Score	**Narrative Focus**	**Organization**	**Development of Narrative**	**Language and Vocabulary**	**Conventions**
4	Narrative is clearly focused and developed throughout.	Narrative has a well-developed, logical, easy-to-follow plot.	Narrative includes thorough and effective use of details, dialogue, and description.	Narrative uses precise, concrete sensory language as well as figurative language and/or domain-specific vocabulary.	Narrative has correct grammar, usage, spelling, capitalization, and punctuation.
3	Narrative is mostly focused and developed throughout.	Narrative has a plot, but there may be some lack of clarity and/or unrelated events.	Narrative includes adequate use of details, dialogue and description.	Narrative uses adequate sensory and figurative language and/or domain-specific vocabulary.	Narrative has a few errors but is completely understandable.
2	Narrative is somewhat developed but may occasionally lose focus.	Narrative's plot is difficult to follow, and ideas are not connected well.	Narrative includes only a few details, dialogues, and descriptions.	Language in narrative is not precise or sensory; lacks domain-specific vocabulary.	Narrative has some errors in usage, grammar, spelling and/or punctuation.
1	Narrative may be confusing, unfocused, or too short.	Narrative has little or no apparent plot.	Narrative includes few or no details, dialogue or description.	Language in narrative is vague, unclear, or confusing.	Narrative is hard to follow because of frequent errors.
0	Narrative gets no credit if it does not demonstrate adequate command of narrative writing traits.				

© **Common Core State Standards**

Writing 3. Write narratives to develop real or imagined experiences or events using effective technique, descriptive details, and clear event sequences. **Writing 9.b.** Apply grade 5 Reading standards to informational texts (e.g., "Explain how an author uses reasons and evidence to support particular points in a text, identifying which reasons and evidence support which point[s]").

Write Like a Reporter
Narrative Scene

Student Prompt Reread the expository text on pp. 352–359 and retell the sequence of events. Pay attention to the investigators' reasoning and take notes on the details, facts, and setting. Then write a scene from a play that dramatizes the investigation. Establish the reindeer herd's situation, and organize the sequence of events logically. Include concrete words and phrases from the text to convey the experience of the investigation.

_____

_____

_____

_____

_____

_____

_____

_____

_____

_____

_____

_____

_____

_____

_____

_____

_____

_____

_____

Write Like a Reporter
Narrative Scene

Student Prompt, p. 170 Reread the expository text on pp. 352–359 and retell the sequence of events. Pay attention to the investigators' reasoning and take notes on the details, facts, and setting. Then write a scene from a play that dramatizes the investigation. Establish the reindeer herd's situation, and organize the sequence of events logically. Include concrete words and phrases from the text to convey the experience of the investigation.

Writing to Sources As students reread, have them make a list of all events as they occur in the text. Have them consider how they would present this information on stage. Before students begin writing, remind them to begin by establishing the situation on the island and to organize events in a way that unfolds naturally. Make sure they use concrete words and phrases from the text to accurately convey the experience of the investigators.

Students' scenes should:

- orient the reader by establishing the situation on Saint Matthew Island
- organize a sequence of events that unfolds naturally
- use concrete words and phrases to convey experiences
- demonstrate strong command of the conventions of standard written English

---

ⓒ **Common Core State Standards**

Writing 3. Write narratives to develop real or imagined experiences or events using effective technique, descriptive details, and clear event sequences. **Writing 9.b.** Apply grade 5 Reading standards to informational texts (e.g., "Explain how an author uses reasons and evidence to support particular points in a text, identifying which reasons and evidence support which point[s]").

Name _____

Connect the Texts
Narrative Article

> **Student Prompt** Look back at *The Mystery of Saint Matthew Island* and "City Hawks" and compare and contrast the factors that threaten the animals' survival. Then write a two-paragraph newspaper article that retells the animals' experiences. Reread both texts carefully to find details to include in your narrative. Remember to organize your narrative so that events unfold naturally and use concrete words and phrases in your descriptions.

_____

_____

_____

_____

_____

_____

_____

_____

_____

_____

_____

_____

_____

_____

_____

_____

_____

Connect the Texts
Narrative Article

Student Prompt, p. 172 Look back at *The Mystery of Saint Matthew Island* and "City Hawks" and compare and contrast the factors that threaten the animals' survival. Then write a two-paragraph newspaper article that retells the animals' experiences. Reread both texts carefully to find details to include in your narrative. Remember to organize your narrative so that events unfold naturally and use concrete words and phrases in your descriptions.

Writing to Sources As students reread, have them make a list of factors that threaten the animals' survival in their habitats. Ask students to compare and contrast these factors. Before students begin writing, remind them to organize their newspaper articles so that the story events unfold in a natural way. Remind them to use concrete words and phrases, as well as details from both texts to convey the animals' experiences.

	4-point Narrative Writing Rubric				
Score	**Narrative Focus**	**Organization**	**Development of Narrative**	**Language and Vocabulary**	**Conventions**
4	Narrative is clearly focused and developed throughout.	Narrative has a well-developed, logical, easy-to-follow plot.	Narrative includes thorough and effective use of details, dialogue, and description.	Narrative uses precise, concrete sensory language as well as figurative language and/or domain-specific vocabulary.	Narrative has correct grammar, usage, spelling, capitalization, and punctuation.
3	Narrative is mostly focused and developed throughout.	Narrative has a plot, but there may be some lack of clarity and/or unrelated events.	Narrative includes adequate use of details, dialogue and description.	Narrative uses adequate sensory and figurative language and/or domain-specific vocabulary.	Narrative has a few errors but is completely understandable.
2	Narrative is somewhat developed but may occasionally lose focus.	Narrative's plot is difficult to follow, and ideas are not connected well.	Narrative includes only a few details, dialogues, and descriptions.	Language in narrative is not precise or sensory; lacks domain-specific vocabulary.	Narrative has some errors in usage, grammar, spelling and/or punctuation.
1	Narrative may be confusing, unfocused, or too short.	Narrative has little or no apparent plot.	Narrative includes few or no details, dialogue or description.	Language in narrative is vague, unclear, or confusing.	Narrative is hard to follow because of frequent errors.
0	Narrative gets no credit if it does not demonstrate adequate command of narrative writing traits.				

© **Common Core State Standards**

Writing 3. Write narratives to develop real or imagined experiences or events using effective technique, descriptive details, and clear event sequences. **Writing 9.b.** Apply grade 5 Reading standards to informational texts (e.g., "Explain how an author uses reasons and evidence to support particular points in a text, identifying which reasons and evidence support which point[s]").

Write Like a Reporter
Narrative Paragraph

Student Prompt Reread the myth on pp. 378–392 and retell the story's plot. Make a list of events as they occur in chronological order and take notes on the details, facts, and setting. Then write a one-paragraph narrative retelling of the story from Aurelia's perspective. Use first-person point of view to introduce Aurelia as the narrator. Organize the events in a natural way, and use narrative techniques, such as dialogue and pacing, to develop events.

_____

_____

_____

_____

_____

_____

_____

_____

_____

_____

_____

_____

_____

_____

_____

_____

Write Like a Reporter
Narrative Paragraph

> **Student Prompt, p. 174** Reread the myth on pp. 378–392 and retell the story's plot. Make a list of events as they occur in chronological order and take notes on the details, facts, and setting. Then write a one-paragraph narrative retelling of the story from Aurelia's perspective. Use first-person point of view to introduce Aurelia as the narrator. Organize the events in a natural way, and use narrative techniques, such as dialogue and pacing, to develop events.

Writing to Sources As students reread, have them make a list of all the events as they occur in the myth. Have them consider how the story would change if it were told from Aurelia's perspective. Before students begin writing, tell them to write their journal entries from a first-person point of view, using *I* instead of *she*. Remind students that their narratives should clearly introduce the narrator and present events in a natural way. The journal entries should also use narrative techniques, such as dialogue and pacing, to develop the plot's events.

Students' paragraphs should:

- introduce Aurelia as the narrator of the narrative retelling
- organize a sequence of events that unfolds naturally
- use narrative techniques, such as dialogue and pacing, to develop events
- demonstrate strong command of the conventions of standard written English

---

© Common Core State Standards

Writing 3. Write narratives to develop real or imagined experiences or events using effective technique, descriptive details, and clear event sequences. **Writing 9.a.** Apply grade 5 Reading standards to literature (e.g., "Compare and contrast two or more characters, settings, or events in a story or a drama, drawing on specific details in the text [e.g., how characters interact]").

Connect the Texts
Narrative Dialogue

Student Prompt Look back at *King Midas and the Golden Touch* and "Prometheus, the Fire-Bringer" and compare and contrast the main characters' attitudes and motivations. Then write a short dialogue between King Midas and Prometheus that reveals each character's main motivation and the outcome of their stories. Reread both texts carefully to find concrete words and phrases and sensory details to include in your narrative.

_____

_____

_____

_____

_____

_____

_____

_____

_____

_____

_____

_____

_____

_____

Connect the Texts
Narrative Dialogue

Student Prompt, p. 176 Look back at *King Midas and the Golden Touch* and "Prometheus, the Fire-Bringer" and compare and contrast the main characters' attitudes and motivations. Then write a short dialogue between King Midas and Prometheus that reveals each character's main motivation and the outcome of their stories. Reread both texts carefully to find concrete words and phrases and sensory details to include in your narrative.

Writing to Sources Before students reread, remind them that *King Midas and the Golden Touch* and "Prometheus, the Fire-Bringer" are myths. Discuss with them the difference between a myth that teaches a lesson (*Midas*) and an origin myth ("Prometheus"). Ask them to reread carefully, paying attention to the characters' motivations and attitudes. Remind students to use concrete words and phrases from both texts in their dialogue.

			4-point Narrative Writing Rubric		
Score	**Narrative Focus**	**Organization**	**Development of Narrative**	**Language and Vocabulary**	**Conventions**
4	Narrative is clearly focused and developed throughout.	Narrative has a well-developed, logical, easy-to-follow plot.	Narrative includes thorough and effective use of details, dialogue, and description.	Narrative uses precise, concrete sensory language as well as figurative language and/or domain-specific vocabulary.	Narrative has correct grammar, usage, spelling, capitalization, and punctuation.
3	Narrative is mostly focused and developed throughout.	Narrative has a plot, but there may be some lack of clarity and/or unrelated events.	Narrative includes adequate use of details, dialogue and description.	Narrative uses adequate sensory and figurative language and/or domain-specific vocabulary.	Narrative has a few errors but is completely understandable.
2	Narrative is somewhat developed but may occasionally lose focus.	Narrative's plot is difficult to follow, and ideas are not connected well.	Narrative includes only a few details, dialogues, and descriptions.	Language in narrative is not precise or sensory; lacks domain-specific vocabulary.	Narrative has some errors in usage, grammar, spelling and/or punctuation.
1	Narrative may be confusing, unfocused, or too short.	Narrative has little or no apparent plot.	Narrative includes few or no details, dialogue or description.	Language in narrative is vague, unclear, or confusing.	Narrative is hard to follow because of frequent errors.
0	Narrative gets no credit if it does not demonstrate adequate command of narrative writing traits.				

Ⓒ **Common Core State Standards**

Writing 3. Write narratives to develop real or imagined experiences or events using effective technique, descriptive details, and clear event sequences. **Writing 9.a.** Apply grade 5 Reading standards to literature (e.g., "Compare and contrast two or more characters, settings, or events in a story or a drama, drawing on specific details in the text [e.g., how characters interact]").

Write Like a Reporter
Narrative Paragraph

Student Prompt Reread the expository text on pp. 416–420 and retell the sequence of events. Pay attention to the chronology of events and take notes on the details, facts, and setting. Then write a one-paragraph postcard telling the story from Werner Franz's perspective. Use a first-person point of view to establish the situation onboard. Organize events in a natural way, and use narrative techniques, such as description and pacing, to develop events.

_____

_____

_____

_____

_____

_____

_____

_____

_____

_____

_____

_____

_____

_____

_____

Write Like a Reporter
Narrative Paragraph

Student Prompt, p. 178 Reread the expository text on pp. 416–420 and retell the sequence of events. Pay attention to the chronology of events and take notes on the details, facts, and setting. Then write a one-paragraph postcard telling the story from Werner Franz's perspective. Use a first-person point of view to establish the situation onboard. Organize events in a natural way, and use narrative techniques, such as description and pacing, to develop events.

Writing to Sources As students reread, have them make a list of all the events as they occur in the expository text. Have them consider how the story would change if it were told from Werner Franz's perspective. Before students begin writing, tell them to write their postcards from a first-person point of view, using *I* instead of *he*. Remind students that their narratives should begin by establishing the situation onboard the *Hindenburg* and to organize the events in a way that unfolds naturally. The postcards should also use narrative techniques, such as description and pacing, to develop events.

Students' paragraphs should:

- orient the reader by establishing the situation onboard
- organize a sequence of events that unfolds naturally
- use narrative techniques, such as description and pacing, to develop events
- demonstrate strong command of the conventions of standard written English

@ **Common Core State Standards**

Writing 3. Write narratives to develop real or imagined experiences or events using effective technique, descriptive details, and clear event sequences. **Writing 9.b.** Apply grade 5 Reading standards to informational texts (e.g., "Explain how an author uses reasons and evidence to support particular points in a text, identifying which reasons and evidence support which point[s]").

Connect the Texts
Narrative Article

Student Prompt Look back at *The* Hindenburg and "The Mystery of the *Hindenburg* Disaster" and compare and contrast the eyewitness accounts given by Helmut Lau and Werner Franz. Then write a short newspaper article that retells the story of the *Hindenburg* disaster using the most effective details. Reread both texts carefully to find concrete words and phrases to include in your narrative.

_____

_____

_____

_____

_____

_____

_____

_____

_____

_____

_____

_____

_____

_____

_____

_____

_____

_____

Connect the Texts
Narrative Article

Student Prompt, p. 180 Look back at *The* Hindenburg and "The Mystery of the *Hindenburg* Disaster" and compare and contrast the eyewitness accounts given by Helmut Lau and Werner Franz. Then write a short newspaper article that retells the story of the *Hindenburg* disaster using the most effective details. Reread both texts carefully to find concrete words and phrases to include in your narrative.

Writing to Sources After students reread, ask them to compare and contrast the accounts of Helmut Lau and Franz Werner. Have them consider which details most effectively capture the disaster. Before students begin writing, remind them to use concrete words and phrases from both texts in their narrative.

4-point Narrative Writing Rubric					
Score	Narrative Focus	Organization	Development of Narrative	Language and Vocabulary	Conventions
4	Narrative is clearly focused and developed throughout.	Narrative has a well-developed, logical, easy-to-follow plot.	Narrative includes thorough and effective use of details, dialogue, and description.	Narrative uses precise, concrete sensory language as well as figurative language and/or domain-specific vocabulary.	Narrative has correct grammar, usage, spelling, capitalization, and punctuation.
3	Narrative is mostly focused and developed throughout.	Narrative has a plot, but there may be some lack of clarity and/or unrelated events.	Narrative includes adequate use of details, dialogue and description.	Narrative uses adequate sensory and figurative language and/or domain-specific vocabulary.	Narrative has a few errors but is completely understandable.
2	Narrative is somewhat developed but may occasionally lose focus.	Narrative's plot is difficult to follow, and ideas are not connected well.	Narrative includes only a few details, dialogues, and descriptions.	Language in narrative is not precise or sensory; lacks domain-specific vocabulary.	Narrative has some errors in usage, grammar, spelling and/or punctuation.
1	Narrative may be confusing, unfocused, or too short.	Narrative has little or no apparent plot.	Narrative includes few or no details, dialogue or description.	Language in narrative is vague, unclear, or confusing.	Narrative is hard to follow because of frequent errors.
0	Narrative gets no credit if it does not demonstrate adequate command of narrative writing traits.				

© Common Core State Standards

Writing 3. Write narratives to develop real or imagined experiences or events using effective technique, descriptive details, and clear event sequences. **Writing 9.b.** Apply grade 5 Reading standards to informational texts (e.g., "Explain how an author uses reasons and evidence to support particular points in a text, identifying which reasons and evidence support which point[s]").

Write Like a Reporter
Narrative Paragraph

Student Prompt Reread the text on pp. 443–451 and retell the sequence of events. Keep track of events as they occur in chronological order, and take notes on the details, facts, and settings. Then write a one-paragraph journal entry from C. J.'s perspective. Use first-person point of view to establish C. J. as the narrator. Use transitions, such as *first*, *next*, and *last*, to clarify the order of events. Also use description and pacing to develop events.

_____

_____

_____

_____

_____

_____

_____

_____

_____

_____

_____

_____

_____

_____

_____

_____

Write Like a Reporter
Narrative Paragraph

> **Student Prompt, p. 182** Reread the text on pp. 443–451 and retell the sequence of events. Keep track of events as they occur in chronological order, and take notes on the details, facts, and settings. Then write a one-paragraph journal entry from C. J.'s perspective. Use first-person point of view to establish C. J. as the narrator. Use transitions, such as *first*, *next*, and *last*, to clarify the order of events. Also use description and pacing to develop events.

Writing to Sources As students reread, have them make a list of all the events as they occur in the text. Before students begin writing, remind them to begin by establishing C. J. as the narrator and to write from a first-person point of view, using *I* instead of *he*. Remind them to use narrative techniques, such as description and pacing, to develop events and to include transitional words to clarify the order of events.

Students' paragraphs should:
- introduce C. J. as the narrator
- use a variety of transitional words to clarify the order of events
- use narrative techniques, such as description and pacing, to develop events
- demonstrate strong command of the conventions of standard written English

---

© Common Core State Standards

Writing 3. Write narratives to develop real or imagined experiences or events using effective technique, descriptive details, and clear event sequences. **Writing 9.a.** Apply grade 5 Reading standards to literature (e.g., "Compare and contrast two or more characters, settings, or events in a story or a drama, drawing on specific details in the text [e.g., how characters interact]").

Connect the Texts
Narrative Dialogue

Student Prompt Look back at *Sweet Music in Harlem* and "Author's Note," and consider the ways author Debbie A. Taylor and fictional character C. J. draw inspiration from the world around them. Then write a short dialogue between the author and the character that reveals how these sources of inspiration influence their creativity. Reread both texts carefully to find concrete words and phrases to include in your narrative.

_____

_____

_____

_____

_____

_____

_____

_____

_____

_____

_____

_____

_____

_____

_____

_____

_____

Connect the Texts
Narrative Dialogue

Student Prompt, p. 184 Look back at *Sweet Music in Harlem* and "Author's Note," and consider the ways author Debbie A. Taylor and fictional character C. J. draw inspiration from the world around them. Then write a short dialogue between the author and the character that reveals how these sources of inspiration influence their creativity. Reread both texts carefully to find concrete words and phrases to include in your narrative.

Writing to Sources Before students reread, remind them that "Author's Note" is an autobiographical account by the author of *Sweet Music in Harlem* that discusses her motivation for writing this piece of realistic fiction. Then have students reread, keeping the theme of inspiration in mind. Discuss with students how Debbie A. Taylor and C. J. draw inspiration from the world around them. Remind students to use concrete words and phrases from both texts in their narratives.

4-point Narrative Writing Rubric					
Score	Narrative Focus	Organization	Development of Narrative	Language and Vocabulary	Conventions
4	Narrative is clearly focused and developed throughout.	Narrative has a well-developed, logical, easy-to-follow plot.	Narrative includes thorough and effective use of details, dialogue, and description.	Narrative uses precise, concrete sensory language as well as figurative language and/or domain-specific vocabulary.	Narrative has correct grammar, usage, spelling, capitalization, and punctuation.
3	Narrative is mostly focused and developed throughout.	Narrative has a plot, but there may be some lack of clarity and/or unrelated events.	Narrative includes adequate use of details, dialogue and description.	Narrative uses adequate sensory and figurative language and/or domain-specific vocabulary.	Narrative has a few errors but is completely understandable.
2	Narrative is somewhat developed but may occasionally lose focus.	Narrative's plot is difficult to follow, and ideas are not connected well.	Narrative includes only a few details, dialogues, and descriptions.	Language in narrative is not precise or sensory; lacks domain-specific vocabulary.	Narrative has some errors in usage, grammar, spelling and/or punctuation.
1	Narrative may be confusing, unfocused, or too short.	Narrative has little or no apparent plot.	Narrative includes few or no details, dialogue or description.	Language in narrative is vague, unclear, or confusing.	Narrative is hard to follow because of frequent errors.
0	Narrative gets no credit if it does not demonstrate adequate command of narrative writing traits.				

© Common Core State Standards

Writing 3. Write narratives to develop real or imagined experiences or events using effective technique, descriptive details, and clear event sequences. **Writing 9.a.** Apply grade 5 Reading standards to literature (e.g., "Compare and contrast two or more characters, settings, or events in a story or a drama, drawing on specific details in the text [e.g., how characters interact]"). **Writing 9.b.** Apply grade 5 Reading standards to informational texts (e.g., "Explain how an author uses reasons and evidence to support particular points in a text, identifying which reasons and evidence support which point[s]").

Prove It!
Narrative Short Story

Dialogue Makes It Happen

Narrative Short Story

In this unit, students have read examples of narrative writing, including a short story, and have had the opportunity to write in this mode. Remind students of texts and writing tasks (such as Write Like a Reporter and Connect the Texts) in which they have encountered and practiced narrative writing.

Key Features of a Short Story

- establishes a setting, a narrator, and characters in the beginning
- includes a clear and logically organized plot, or sequence of events
- includes dialogue, pacing, and details to develop events and characters
- uses transition words, phrases, and clauses to show sequence
- uses precise words and phrases, descriptive details, and sensory language
- has a conclusion that follows from the events

Writing Task Overview

Each unit writing task provides students with an opportunity to write to sources. To successfully complete the task, students must analyze, synthesize, and evaluate multiple complex texts and create their own written response.

Dialogue Makes It Happen

Part 1: Students will reread and take notes on the selected sources. They will then respond to several questions about these sources and discuss their written responses with partners or in small groups.

Part 2: Students will work individually to plan, write, and revise their own short story.

Scorable Products: short responses, short story

Dialogue Makes It Happen: Writing Task – Short Response

Teacher Directions:

1. **Introduce the Sources** Refer students to the following texts in the Student Edition:

    1. *King Midas and the Golden Touch,* pp. 376–393

    2. "Prometheus, the Fire-Bringer," pp. 398–399

    3. *Sweet Music in Harlem,* pp. 440–457

    Explain to students that they will need to draw evidence and support from the texts above in order to answer evidence-based short response questions and to write a short story. Students should take notes on narrative structures and elements as they closely reread the texts. Students should be given paper or a relevant graphic organizer from the TR DVD for note-taking.

2. **Provide Student Directions and Scoring Information (p. 190)** Answer any task-related questions students may have. If necessary, provide additional paper for students to write their responses.

3. **Initiate the Writing Task** If you are timing this part of the task, you may wish to alert students when half the allotted time has elapsed and again when 5 minutes remain.

4. **Facilitate Collaboration** After students have completed their written responses to the evidence-based short response questions, assign partners or small groups and have them discuss their responses. If students struggle to work together productively, provide them with tips and strategies for summarizing the points a

Ⓒ Common Core State Standards

Writing 3. Write narratives to develop real or imagined experiences or events using effective technique, descriptive details, and clear event sequences. **Speaking/Listening 1.** Engage effectively in a range of collaborative discussions (one-on-one, in groups, and teacher-led) with diverse partners on grade 5 topics and texts, building on others' ideas and expressing their own clearly. **(Also Writing 3.a., Writing 3.b., Writing 3.c., Writing 3.d., Writing 3.e.)**

Scoring Information

Use the following 2-point scoring rubrics to evaluate students' answers to the evidence-based short response questions.

1. Compare and contrast how the authors of *King Midas and the Golden Touch,* "Prometheus, the Fire-Bringer," and *Sweet Music in Harlem* describe what happens. Use details from each source to identify the main events and explain how the plots are and are not alike.

	Analysis Rubric
2	The response: • demonstrates the ability to analyze similarities and differences between the plot presentation and main events in texts • includes specific details that make reference to the texts
1	The response: • demonstrates a limited ability to analyze similarities and differences between the plot presentation and main events in texts • includes some details that make reference to the texts
0	A response receives no credit if it demonstrates no ability to analyze similarities and differences between the techniques or includes no relevant details from the texts.

2. Draw a conclusion about how dialogue helps to show what happens in all three stories. Cite details and examples from the sources to support your response.

	Synthesis Rubric
2	The response: • demonstrates the ability to synthesize information from the sources in order to draw a conclusion about dialogue • includes specific details that make reference to the texts
1	The response: • demonstrates a limited ability to synthesize information from the sources in order to draw a conclusion about dialogue • includes some details that make reference to the texts
0	A response receives no credit if it demonstrates no ability to synthesize information from the sources or includes no relevant details from the texts.

3. Decide which story uses dialogue most effectively to reveal what happens. Explain your judgment of the best use of dialogue by referring to quotations and details from each story.

Evaluation Rubric		
2		The response: • demonstrates the ability to evaluate the effective use of dialogue • includes specific details that make reference to the texts
1		The response: • demonstrates a limited ability to evaluate the effective use of dialogue • includes some details that make reference to the texts
0		A response receives no credit if it demonstrates no ability to evaluate the effective use of dialogue or includes no relevant details from the texts.

ⓒ **Common Core State Standards**

Writing 8. Recall relevant information from experiences or gather relevant information from print and digital sources; summarize or paraphrase information in notes and finished work, and provide a list of sources. **Writing 9.** Draw evidence from literary or informational texts to support analysis, reflection, and research.

Dialogue Makes It Happen
Writing Task – Short Response

Student Directions:

Your Assignment   You will reread three selections from Unit 6 and take notes on these sources. Then you will answer three questions about these materials. You may refer to your notes or to any of the sources as often as you like.

Sources

1. *King Midas and the Golden Touch,* pp. 376–393

2. "Prometheus, the Fire-Bringer," pp. 398–399

3. *Sweet Music in Harlem,* pp. 440–457

Be sure to read closely and take good notes. Your sources and notes will be the basis for writing your own short story in the second half of this writing task.

Evidence-Based Short Response Questions   Answer the short response questions on the lines provided below each question. Your answers to these questions will be scored. Be sure to base your answers on the sources you have just read. Remember that you may refer back to your notes or to any of the sources.

After you have answered the questions, you will discuss your responses with a partner or within a small group. Your teacher will let you know when to begin the discussion part of this task.

Scoring Information   Your responses will be scored based on how well you demonstrate the ability to:

- compare information across texts
- include specific details and examples from the sources
- analyze, synthesize, and evaluate information
- distinguish key details from unnecessary information

Evidence-Based Short Response Questions

1. Compare and contrast how the authors of *King Midas and the Golden Touch*, "Prometheus, the Fire-Bringer," and *Sweet Music in Harlem* describe what happens. Use details from each source to identify the main events and explain how the plots are and are not alike.

_____

_____

_____

_____

2. Draw a conclusion about how dialogue helps to show what happens in all three stories. Cite details and examples from the sources to support your response.

_____

_____

_____

_____

3. Decide which story uses dialogue most effectively to reveal what happens. Explain your judgment of the best use of dialogue by referring to quotations and details from each story.

_____

_____

_____

_____

Collaborative Discussion

After you have written your responses to the questions, discuss your ideas. Your teacher will assign you a partner or a small group and let you know when to begin.

Dialogue Makes It Happen: Writing Task – Short Story

Teacher Directions:

1. **Provide Student Directions and Scoring Information (p. 194)** Explain to students that they will now review their notes and sources, and plan, draft, and revise their short stories. Although they may use their notes and sources, they must work alone. Students will be allowed to look back at the answers they wrote to the short response questions, but they will not be allowed to make changes to those answers. Have students read the directions for the short story and answer any task-related questions they may have. Students should be given paper on which to write their short stories.

2. **Initiate the Writing Task** If you are timing this part of the task, you may wish to suggest approximate times for students to begin writing and revising. If students wish to continue writing rather than revising, allow them to do so. Alert students when 5 minutes remain.

3. **Scoring Information** Use the scoring rubric on the next page to evaluate students' short stories.

4. **Short Story Prompt** Use what you have learned to rewrite an important scene from one of the selections you have read. In the rewritten scene, replace the main character with a different character from one of the other stories. Think about how that character will behave in the situation. Tell most of what happens by means of dialogue. Make use of precise language, details, and sensory language.

4-point Narrative Writing Rubric					
Score	**Narrative Focus**	**Organization**	**Development of Narrative**	**Language and Vocabulary**	**Conventions**
4	Short story is clearly focused and developed throughout.	Short story has a well-developed, logical, easy-to-follow plot.	Short story includes thorough and effective use of details, dialogue, and description.	Short story uses precise, concrete sensory language as well as figurative language.	Short story has correct grammar, usage, spelling, capitalization, and punctuation.
3	Short story is mostly focused and developed throughout.	Short story has a plot, but there may be some lack of clarity and/or unrelated events.	Short story includes adequate use of details, dialogue, and description.	Short story uses adequate sensory and figurative language.	Short story has a few errors but is completely understandable.
2	Short story is somewhat developed but may occasionally lose focus.	Short story's plot is difficult to follow, and ideas are not connected well.	Short story includes only a few details, dialogues, and descriptions.	Language in short story is not concrete, precise, or sensory.	Short story has some errors in usage, grammar, spelling, and/or punctuation.
1	Short story may be confusing, unfocused, or too short.	Short story has little or no apparent plot.	Short story includes few or no details, dialogue, and description.	Language in short story is vague, unclear, or confusing.	Short story is hard to follow because of frequent errors.
0	Short story gets no credit if it does not demonstrate adequate command of narrative writing traits.				

Ⓒ Common Core State Standards

Writing 3. Write narratives to develop real or imagined experiences or events using effective technique, descriptive details, and clear event sequences. **Writing 9.** Draw evidence from literary or informational texts to support analysis, reflection, and research. (**Also Writing 3.a.,** **Writing 3.b., Writing 3.c., Writing 10.**)

Dialogue Makes It Happen
Writing Task – Short Story

Student Directions:

Your Assignment Now you will review your notes and sources, and plan, draft, and revise your short story. While you may use your notes and refer to the sources, you must work on your own. You may also refer to the answers you wrote to earlier questions, but you cannot change those answers.

Short Story Prompt Use what you have learned to rewrite an important scene from one of the selections you have read. In the rewritten scene, replace the main character with a different character from one of the other stories. Think about how that character will behave in the situation. Tell most of what happens by means of dialogue. Make use of precise language, details, and sensory language.

Scoring Information Your short story will be assigned a score for

1. **Focus** – how well you create a situation and introduce the narrator and characters

2. **Organization** – how well you organize a clear order of events, using transitions to show sequence

3. **Elaboration** – how well you use dialogue and description to reveal and develop events and characters

4. **Language and Vocabulary** – how well you use precise words, details, and sensory language

5. **Conventions** – how well you follow the rules of grammar, usage, capitalization, punctuation, and spelling

Now begin work on your short story. Try to manage your time carefully so that you can

- plan your short story
- write your short story
- revise and edit for a final draft

Dialogue Makes It Happen: Writing Task – Short Story

Teacher Directions:

1. Publish Explain to students that publishing their writing is the last step in the writing process. If time permits, have students review one another's short stories and incorporate any comments their classmates have. Offer students suggestions for how to publish their work in an online magazine or a presentation that may include props, costumes, and sound effects.

2. Present Students will now have the option to present their short stories. Have students give dramatic readings of their short stories in front of the class. Use the list below to offer students some tips on listening and speaking.

While Listening to a Classmate...

- Keep your focus on what the speaker is saying.
- Try to visualize what is happening. Create mental pictures of the characters.

While Speaking to Classmates...

- Vary your voice to show different characters and different tones.
- Vary your pace to build excitement or suspense.
- Use body language and sound effects to add drama and keep your audience interested.

Things to Do Together...

- Keep the purpose in mind: your role is to entertain or to be entertained.
- Make comments that contribute to the discussion and build on others' ideas.
- Follow agreed-upon rules for discussions. Avoid interrupting a speaker.

© Common Core State Standards

Writing 6. With some guidance and support from adults, use technology, including the Internet, to produce and publish writing as well as to interact and collaborate with others; demonstrate sufficient command of keyboarding skills to type a minimum of two pages in a single sitting. **Speaking/Listening 1.b.** Follow agreed-upon rules for discussions and carry out assigned roles. **Speaking/Listening 5.** Include multimedia components (graphics, sound) and visual displays in presentations when appropriate to enhance the development or main ideas or themes. **Speaking/Listening 6.** Adapt speech to a variety of contexts and tasks, using formal English when appropriate to the task and situation.

More Connect the Texts

Public Safety Advertisement

Objectives

- Identify the characteristics of a public safety advertisement.
- Write a public safety advertisement, using facts and supporting details.
- Evaluate your writing.
- Revise and publish your writing.

Ⓒ Common Core State Standards

Writing 1. Write opinion pieces on topics or texts, supporting a point of view with reasons and information. **Writing 4.** Produce clear and coherent writing in which the development and organization are appropriate to task, purpose, and audience. **Writing 5.** With guidance and support from peers and adults, develop and strengthen writing as needed by planning, revising, editing, rewriting, or trying a new approach. **Writing 6.** With some guidance and support from adults, use technology, including the Internet, to produce and publish writing as well as to interact and collaborate with others; demonstrate sufficient command of keyboarding skills to type a minimum of two pages in a single sitting. **Writing 8.** Recall relevant information from experiences or gather relevant information from print and digital sources; summarize or paraphrase information in notes and finished work, and provide a list of sources. **Writing 9.** Draw evidence from literary or informational texts to support analysis, reflection, and research.

STEP 1 Read Like a Writer

Review the key features of a public safety advertisement listed below. Respond to any questions students might have.

Key Features of a Public Safety Advertisement

- States the writer's point of view, opinion, or claim
- Tries to influence the reader's opinion, or claim, by developing an argument supported by reasons and information
- Provides logically ordered evidence that is supported by facts, details, and examples
- Provides a conclusion that is related to the opinion, or claim, presented
- Urges the reader to take action

Choose an argumentative or persuasive text that students have already read to model key features. Display the model for students to see and point out each of the key features you have discussed.

STEP 2 Organize Your Ideas

Writing Prompt Look back at "What Will I Do in an Emergency?" and "Seven Survival Questions." Both texts discuss the steps to take in emergency situations. Being prepared for emergencies can make the difference between surviving and not surviving. Write a public safety advertisement designed to convince hikers to prepare for possible emergencies when planning wilderness hikes. Use evidence from each text to support your opinion, or claim.

Think Aloud Your ideas will be more convincing if they are well organized and presented in a logical order. Decide on the opinion, or claim, you will state in your advertisement. Then, decide what facts, details, and examples you will draw from "What Will I Do in an Emergency?" and "Seven Survival Questions" to support your opinion, or claim.

Guided Writing Display an outline as an example. Help students organize the ideas that support their opinion, or claim, into an outline. Explain to them that they will write a paragraph for each idea, with the main point conveyed in the topic sentence. Each paragraph will include facts and details that support the topic sentence.

STEP 3 Draft Your Writing

Have students use their outlines to write a public safety advertisement. Remind them of the key features of a public safety advertisement.

Think Aloud One of the best ways to persuade readers is to use facts and details that support your opinion, or claim. Gather facts and details from "What Will I Do in an Emergency?" and "Seven Survival Questions." You can also use books, articles, and Web sites to find additional facts and details.

Getting Started Tell students to begin writing their public safety advertisement using their outlines to keep them on track. Give them suggestions on where to place their facts and supporting details. Emphasize the importance of using correct grammar, precise language, and complete sentences. Remind them to end with a concluding statement related to the opinion, or claim, presented.

STEP 4 Evaluate Your Writing

Display the checklist below and have students use it to evaluate their public safety advertisements. Circulate around the room and confer with individual students.

✓ Is my opinion, or claim, clearly stated in a topic sentence?
✓ Did I include facts, details, and examples to persuade my readers?
✓ Is my essay organized in a logical way?
✓ Did I use precise language and complete sentences?
✓ Does my concluding statement make sense?

Help students set goals and a plan for improving their writing as needed.

STEP 5 Revise and Publish

Help students follow through with their plans for revision. If time permits, have students trade advertisements and offer up suggestions for how to improve their writing.

Publishing Students can set up a class blog and post their advertisements for friends and family members to read and comment on.

Nomination Letter

Objectives

- Identify the characteristics of a nomination letter.
- Write a nomination letter, using facts and concrete details.
- Evaluate your writing.
- Revise and publish your writing.

Ⓒ Common Core State Standards

Writing 1. Write opinion pieces on topics or texts, supporting a point of view with reasons and information. **Writing 4.** Produce clear and coherent writing in which the development and organization are appropriate to task, purpose, and audience. **Writing 5.** With guidance and support from peers and adults, develop and strengthen writing as needed by planning, revising, editing, rewriting, or trying a new approach. **Writing 6.** With some guidance and support from adults, use technology, including the Internet, to produce and publish writing as well as to interact and collaborate with others; demonstrate sufficient command of keyboarding skills to type a minimum of two pages in a single sitting. **Writing 9.** Draw evidence from literary or informational texts to support analysis, reflection, and research.

STEP 1 Read Like a Writer

Review the key features of a nomination letter listed below. Respond to any questions students might have.

Key Features of a Nomination Letter

- States the writer's point of view, opinion, or claim
- Tries to influence the reader's opinion, or claim, by developing an argument supported by reasons and information
- Provides logically ordered evidence in the form of facts, concrete details, and examples
- Provides a conclusion that is related to the opinions, or claims, presented
- Urges the reader to take action

Choose an argumentative or persuasive text that students have already read to model key features. Display the model for students to see and point out each of the key features you have discussed.

STEP 2 Organize Your Ideas

Writing Prompt In *The Chí-lin Purse* and *A Summer's Trade,* the main characters give up something of their own to help someone else. Write a nomination letter telling why Hsiang-ling and Tony should be honored with awards for their actions. Use evidence from the texts to support your argument.

Think Aloud Your task is to convince a committee that Hsiang-ling and Tony deserve awards in recognition of the sacrifices they made for others. Reread each selection and make a list of each character's actions. Include facts and concrete details about the good deeds and about how the deeds helped someone else. You will use the facts and details to support your claim that Hsiang-ling and Tony deserve awards.

Guided Writing Help students use an outline to organize the details in their lists. Remind them that they are writing a single letter for both characters. Encourage them to find common themes in the actions of Hsiang-ling and Tony that they can use to support their claim. Explain that they should begin their letters with a strong topic sentence that states their claim and links the two characters. They will then use one or more paragraphs to provide details about each character and his or her actions. They will end their letters with a concluding statement that restates their claim that Hsiang-ling and Tony deserve awards.

STEP 3 Draft Your Writing

Have students use their outlines to write a nomination letter. Remind them of the key features of a nomination letter.

Think Aloud Remember that a nomination letter is meant to persuade the reader. One of the best ways to persuade readers is to use facts and details that support your opinion or claim. Use concrete details from *The Chí-lin Purse* and *A Summer's Trade* to support your claim.

Getting Started Tell students to begin writing their nomination letters using their outlines to keep them on track. Give them suggestions on common themes and on where to include more information and concrete details. Encourage them to use words, phrases, and clauses to link their opinions and their reasons. Emphasize the importance of using correct grammar, precise language, and complete sentences. Remind them to end with a concluding statement related to their claim.

STEP 4 Evaluate Your Writing

Display the checklist below and have students use it to evaluate their nomination letter. Circulate around the room and confer with individual students.

- ✓ Is my position clearly stated in a topic sentence?
- ✓ Did I include facts, details, and examples to persuade my readers?
- ✓ Is my letter organized in a logical way?
- ✓ Did I use complete sentences, precise language, and correct grammar?
- ✓ Did I use appropriate words, phrases, and clauses to link my opinions and reasons?
- ✓ Does my concluding statement reinforce my claim?

Help students set goals and a plan for improving their writing as needed.

STEP 5 Revise and Publish

Help students follow through with their plans for revision. If time permits, have students trade letters and offer suggestions for how to improve their writing.

Publishing Have students type their letters on a computer and invite friends and family members to read and comment on them.

Persuasive Speech

Objectives

- Identify the characteristics of a persuasive speech.
- Write a persuasive speech, using facts and supporting details to support your position.
- Evaluate your writing.
- Revise and publish your writing.

© Common Core State Standards

Writing 1. Write opinion pieces on topics or texts, supporting a point of view with reasons and information. **Writing 4.** Produce clear and coherent writing in which the development and organization are appropriate to task, purpose, and audience. **Writing 5.** With guidance and support from peers and adults, develop and strengthen writing as needed by planning, revising, editing, rewriting, or trying a new approach. **Writing 9.** Draw evidence from literary or informational texts to support analysis, reflection, and research.

STEP 1 Read Like a Writer

Review the key features of a persuasive speech that are listed below. Respond to any questions students might have.

Key Features of a Persuasive Speech

- Attempts to get support for an idea
- Clearly states a position at the beginning of the speech
- States the main idea in the topic sentence of each paragraph
- Uses words, phrases, and clauses to link opinions with reasons
- Provides evidence that is supported by facts, details, and examples
- Presents evidence in order of importance
- Provides a conclusion that reinforces the position taken

Choose a persuasive speech that students have already read to model key features. Display the model for students to see and point out each of the key features you have discussed.

STEP 2 Organize Your Ideas

Writing Prompt Look back at *Weslandia* and *Tripping Over the Lunch Lady*. Wesley and Jinx both have traits that make them different from the people around them. Both come to happily accept their differences. Use details from the two stories to write a persuasive speech about the importance of realizing that it is okay to be different.

Think Aloud Persuasive speeches are meant to sway people to your way of thinking. Thus, you need to include convincing evidence and present the evidence in a logical way. Persuasive speeches often arrange evidence in order of importance. Reread *Weslandia* and *Tripping Over the Lunch Lady* to find evidence that supports your claim that it is important for people to appreciate their differences.

Guided Writing Suggest that students use an outline to organize their evidence in order of importance. Display an outline as an example. Help students order their evidence. Explain to them that they will write an introductory paragraph that states their position. They will use the body of the speech to present evidence in order of importance. They will conclude their speech with a statement that reinforces their position.

STEP 3 Draft Your Writing

Have students use their outlines to write a persuasive speech. Remind them of the key features of a persuasive speech.

Think Aloud One of the best ways to persuade readers is to use facts and details that support your opinion. Gather facts and details from the stories. Order them so that they build a strong argument.

Getting Started Tell students to begin writing their speeches using their outlines to keep them on track. Give them suggestions on how to order their facts and supporting details. Emphasize the importance of using correct grammar and complete sentences. Remind them to end with a concluding statement that reinforces their position.

STEP 4 Evaluate Your Writing

Display the checklist below and have students use it to evaluate their persuasive speeches. Circulate around the room and confer with individual students.

- ✓ Is my position clearly stated in the introduction?
- ✓ Did I include facts, details, and examples to persuade my audience?
- ✓ Are my reasons organized in order of importance?
- ✓ Did I use appropriate words, phrases, and clauses to link my opinions and reasons?
- ✓ Did I use complete sentences and correct grammar?
- ✓ Does my concluding statement reinforce my position?

Help students set goals and develop a plan for improving their writing as needed.

STEP 5 Revise and Publish

Help students follow through with their plans for revision. If time permits, have students trade speeches and offer suggestions for how to improve their writing.

Publishing Have students present their speeches in small groups or in front of the class.

Persuasive Advertisement

Objectives

- Identify the characteristics of a persuasive advertisement.
- Write an advertisement using persuasive words and language that appeals to emotion.
- Evaluate your writing.
- Revise and publish your writing.

Common Core State Standards

Writing 1. Write opinion pieces on topics or texts, supporting a point of view with reasons and information. **Writing 4.** Produce clear and coherent writing in which the development and organization are appropriate to task, purpose, and audience. **Writing 5.** With guidance and support from peers and adults, develop and strengthen writing as needed by planning, revising, editing, rewriting, or trying a new approach. **Writing 6.** With some guidance and support from adults, use technology, including the Internet, to produce and publish writing as well as to interact and collaborate with others; demonstrate sufficient command of keyboarding skills to type a minimum of two pages in a single sitting. **Writing 9.** Draw evidence from literary or informational texts to support analysis, reflection, and research.

STEP 1 Read Like a Writer

Review the key features of a persuasive advertisement listed below. Respond to any questions students might have.

Key Features of a Persuasive Advertisement

- Grabs readers' attention
- Takes a position about a product, service, or idea
- Uses details to urge readers to take action or make a purchase

Choose a print or online advertisement to model the key features. Display the model for students to see and point out each of the key features you have discussed.

STEP 2 Organize Your Ideas

Writing Prompt In "Books and Adventure," Lenny Jackson and Danny Tomzak become friends and share adventure at Camp Caribou. *Ghost Towns of the American West* tells about countless people who headed west in hopes of striking it rich or starting new lives. Use information from the selections to create an advertisement to convince Lenny and Danny to head west during the Gold Rush.

Think Aloud Persuasive ads try to quickly grab your attention, often by appealing to your emotions. Their goal is to get you to take action or make a purchase. Work with a partner to create your advertisement. Reread "Books and Adventure" and *Ghost Towns of the American West* to find details to include in your advertisements. Use a T-chart to collect your details. List details about the characters of Lenny and Danny on one side. What do you know about them that would make them want to go west? List details from *Ghost Towns of the American West* on the other side that you think would appeal to Lenny and Danny.

Guided Writing Work with students to identify details in both selections that will help persuade Lenny and Danny to take action. Help them organize main ideas and supporting details into an outline. Tell students that their advertisements should begin with an attention-grabbing statement. They should then establish a position that appeals to the emotions of Lenny and Danny. Finally they should use concrete details to influence their target audience.

STEP 3 Draft Your Writing

Have students use their outlines to write their advertisements. Remind them of the key features of a persuasive advertisement.

Think Aloud One of the best ways to persuade readers is to use facts and details that support your opinion but also appeal to emotions. Gather facts and details from the two selections. Think about how to best use the details to influence your audience.

Getting Started Tell students to begin writing their advertisements using their outlines to keep them on track. Give them suggestions on how best to use the details to influence Lenny and Danny. Emphasize the importance of using correct grammar. Encourage them to use time-order words to build their argument.

STEP 4 Evaluate Your Writing

Display the checklist below and have students use it to evaluate their advertisements. Circulate around the room and confer with individual students.

✓ Did I begin with an attention-grabbing statement?
✓ Did I establish a position that appeals to the emotions of my target audience?
✓ Did I use supporting details to influence Lenny and Danny to go west?
✓ Did I use time-order words to help organize my argument?

Help students set goals and a plan for improving their writing as needed.

STEP 5 Revise and Publish

Help students follow through with their plans for revision. If time permits, have students trade advertisements and offer suggestions for how to improve their writing.

Publishing Students can present their advertisements as illustrated posters.

Problem-Solution Essay

Objectives

- Identify the characteristics of a problem-solution essay.
- Write a problem-solution essay using facts and supporting details.
- Evaluate your writing.
- Revise and publish your writing.

Ⓒ Common Core State Standards

Writing 1. Write opinion pieces on topics or texts, supporting a point of view with reasons and information. **Writing 4.** Produce clear and coherent writing in which the development and organization are appropriate to task, purpose, and audience. **Writing 5.** With guidance and support from peers and adults, develop and strengthen writing as needed by planning, revising, editing, rewriting, or trying a new approach. **Writing 6.** With some guidance and support from adults, use technology, including the Internet, to produce and publish writing as well as to interact and collaborate with others; demonstrate sufficient command of keyboarding skills to type a minimum of two pages in a single sitting. **Writing 9.** Draw evidence from literary or informational texts to support analysis, reflection, and research.

STEP 1 Read Like a Writer

Review the key features of a problem-solution essay listed below. Respond to any questions students might have.

Key Features of a Problem-Solution Essay

- Clearly establishes the problem
- Includes opinions and solutions supported by logically ordered facts, details, and examples
- Provides a conclusion that is related to the opinion presented
- Uses a persuasive tone and often urges the reader to take action

Choose a problem-solution essay or argumentative/persuasive text that students have already read to model key features. Display the model for students to see and point out each of the key features you have discussed.

STEP 2 Organize Your Ideas

Writing Prompt In *The Truth About Austin's Amazing Bats* and "City Hawks," people react negatively to the presence of bats and red-tailed hawks in the city. Use evidence from the two selections to write a problem-solution essay arguing that peaceful coexistence is the best solution to the problem of wild animals in cities.

Think Aloud Use a problem-solution chart to collect evidence from each selection for your essay. You want to collect evidence that will support your position that living peacefully with wild animals is the best solution. Look for evidence that shows the benefits provided by the animals, such as mosquito control in the case of bats.

Guided Writing Help students organize the evidence they collect. Explain that they will begin their essay by clearly stating the problem and solution. The paragraphs that follow will use the facts and details gathered from the selections to persuade readers to agree with the solution. The essay should end with a concluding statement that calls for readers to accept the presence of wildlife in the city.

STEP 3 Draft Your Writing

Have students use their charts to write a problem-solution essay. Remind them of the key features of a problem-solution essay.

Think Aloud You will want to begin by stating your problem and solution as clearly as possible. Be sure to link your opinions to reasons by providing facts and details that support your position. Your goal is to convince your readers to accept your solution and take action. Using persuasive words will help you do this.

Getting Started Tell students to begin writing their problem-solution essays using their charts to keep them on track. Give them suggestions on where to place their facts and supporting details for best effect. Emphasize the importance of using correct grammar and complete sentences. Remind students to use a persuasive tone and end with a call to action.

STEP 4 Evaluate Your Writing

Display the checklist below and have students use it to evaluate their problem-solution essays. Circulate around the room and confer with individual students.

✓ Did I clearly establish my position about the problem?

✓ Did I use facts, details, and explanations to support my opinions and solution?

✓ Is my essay organized in a logical way?

✓ Did I use complete sentences and correct grammar?

✓ Did I use a persuasive tone?

✓ Did I end with a call to action?

Help students set goals and a plan for improving in areas where their writing needs to be strengthened.

STEP 5 Revise and Publish

Help students follow through with their plans for revision. If time permits, have students trade problem-solution essays and offer suggestions for how to improve their writing.

Publishing Students can set up a class blog and post their essays for friends and family members to read and comment on.

More Connect the Texts
Opinion Piece

Objectives

- Identify the characteristics of an opinion piece.
- Write an opinion piece using facts and supporting details.
- Evaluate your writing.
- Revise and publish your writing.

© Common Core State Standards

Writing 1. Write opinion pieces on topics or texts, supporting a point of view with reasons and information. **Writing 4.** Produce clear and coherent writing in which the development and organization are appropriate to task, purpose, and audience. **Writing 5.** With guidance and support from peers and adults, develop and strengthen writing as needed by planning, revising, editing, rewriting, or trying a new approach. **Writing 6.** With some guidance and support from adults, use technology, including the Internet, to produce and publish writing as well as to interact and collaborate with others; demonstrate sufficient command of keyboarding skills to type a minimum of two pages in a single sitting. **Writing 9.** Draw evidence from literary or informational texts to support analysis, reflection, and research.

STEP 1 Read Like a Writer

Review the key features of an opinion piece listed below. Respond to any questions students might have.

Key Features of an Opinion Piece

- States the writer's opinion, or claim
- Provides evidence that is supported by facts, details, and examples
- Follows an appropriate and logically organized structure
- Contains a clear topic sentence that is supported by specific facts, definitions, concrete details, quotations, examples, or other information
- Provides a concluding statement related to the opinion presented

Choose an opinion piece that students have already read to model key features. Display the model for students to see and point out each of the key features you have discussed.

STEP 2 Organize Your Ideas

Writing Prompt Look back at "Roberto Clemente: A Baseball Hero" and *Ten Mile Day*. Clemente and the railroad workers faced personal challenges in achieving their goals. Write an essay that gives your opinion about who faced the greater challenges. Support your topic by citing evidence from each text.

Think Aloud Your ideas will be more convincing if they are well organized and presented in a logical order. Before you begin writing, list the challenges Clemente and the railroad workers faced. You may want to use a chart to organize the details. Then decide the order in which you want to discuss the challenges. It can help to make an outline before you write.

Guided Writing Display an outline as an example. Help students organize their information into an outline. Explain that they will organize the challenges of Clemente in one paragraph and the challenges of the railroad workers in another paragraph. Each paragraph will convey the main idea in the topic sentence and include facts, definitions, details, quotations, and other information that support the topic sentence. Finally, students will need to state their opinions and include supporting details.

STEP 3 Draft Your Writing

Have students use their charts and outlines to write an opinion piece. Remind them of the key features of an opinion piece.

Think Aloud Remember that, in an opinion piece, the writer backs up a claim with supporting evidence. You will be using your chart or list as you write the draft of your essay.

Getting Started Tell students to begin writing their essays using their outlines to keep them on track. Give them guidance on where to place facts and details that support their opinions. Emphasize the importance of using precise language, correct grammar, and complete sentences. Remind them to end with a concluding statement about their opinion.

STEP 4 Evaluate Your Writing

Display the checklist below and have students use it to evaluate their opinion pieces. Circulate around the room and confer with individual students.

✓ Did I clearly state the personal challenges?

✓ Did I include facts and concrete details?

✓ Is my essay organized in a logical way?

✓ Did I state my opinion and back it up with evidence?

✓ Did I use complete sentences?

✓ Does my concluding sentence make sense?

Help students set goals and a plan for improving their writing as needed.

STEP 5 Revise and Publish

Help students follow through with their plans for revision. If time permits, have students trade essays and offer suggestions for how to improve their writing.

Publishing Students can e-mail their essays to family and friends.

Persuasive Essay

Objectives

- Identify the characteristics of a persuasive essay.
- Write a persuasive essay using facts and supporting details.
- Evaluate your writing.
- Revise and publish your writing.

Ⓒ Common Core State Standards

Writing 1. Write arguments to support claims with reasons and relevant evidence.
Writing 4. Produce clear and coherent writing in which the development and organization are appropriate to task, purpose, and audience.
Writing 5. With guidance and support from peers and adults, develop and strengthen writing as needed by planning, revising, editing, rewriting, or trying a new approach.
Writing 6. With some guidance and support from adults, use technology, including the Internet, to produce and publish writing as well as to interact and collaborate with others; demonstrate sufficient command of keyboarding skills to type a minimum of two pages in a single sitting.
Writing 9. Draw evidence from literary or informational texts to support analysis, reflection, and research.

STEP 1 Read Like a Writer

Review the key features of a persuasive essay listed below. Respond to any questions students might have.

Key Features of a Persuasive Essay

- Tries to influence the reader's opinion by developing an argument
- Provides evidence that is supported by facts, details, and examples
- Often urges the reader to take action
- Contains a conclusion that is directly related to the opinion, or claim

Choose a persuasive essay that students have already read to model key features. Display the model for students to see and point out each of the key features you have discussed.

STEP 2 Organize Your Ideas

Writing Prompt Look back at "The Eagle and the Bat" and "Thunderbird and Killer Whale." Both texts involve a clever character who fails to achieve his goal. Use evidence from each myth to write a persuasive essay in which you explain whether the bat or Thunderbird came to a worse end. Support your claim by citing concrete details from each text.

Think Aloud Before you begin writing, complete a sequence graphic organizer for each myth. List the events chronologically. Reread the two selections to find specific facts and details about what happens. This will help you recall the events of each text and decide which character came to a worse end.

Guided Writing Encourage students to use an outline to organize their essays. Display an outline as an example. Help students use details from their graphic organizers to develop their outlines. Explain that they will begin the essay by clearly stating their opinion, or claim, in the introduction. They will then provide details from both texts to support the claim. They will conclude their essay with a statement that reiterates their claim.

STEP 3 Draft Your Writing

Have students use their outlines to write a persuasive essay. Remind them of the key features of a persuasive essay.

Think Aloud One of the best ways to persuade readers is to use details that support your claim. Try using a quote from a text. Use this sentence starter: In the myth, the author writes, "(insert quotation)."

Getting Started Tell students to begin writing their persuasive essays using their outlines to keep them on track. Give them guidance on where to place supporting details that illustrate their claims. Emphasize the importance of using correct grammar and complete sentences. Remind them to use words, phrases, and clauses that make their claims clear.

STEP 4 Evaluate Your Writing

Display the checklist below and have students use it to evaluate their persuasive essays. Circulate around the room and confer with individual students.

✓ Did I clearly state my claim in the introduction?
✓ Did I include concrete details that support my claim?
✓ Is my essay organized in a logical way?
✓ Did I use words, phrases, and clauses that make my claim clear?
✓ Did I use complete sentences?
✓ Does my concluding sentence follow logically from my claim?

Help students set goals and a plan for improving their writing as needed.

STEP 5 Revise and Publish

Help students follow through with their plans for revision. If time permits, have students trade essays and offer suggestions for how to improve their writing.

Publishing Students can read their persuasive essays aloud and discuss how the process of writing their essays helped them to better understand the myths. They can then compile the essays on a CD or DVD.

More Connect the Texts
Persuasive Essay

Objectives

- Identify the characteristics of a persuasive essay.
- Write a persuasive essay using persuasive words and clear language.
- Evaluate your writing.
- Revise and publish your writing.

Ⓒ Common Core State Standards

Writing 1. Write opinion pieces on topics or texts, supporting a point of view with reasons and information. **Writing 4.** Produce clear and coherent writing in which the development and organization are appropriate to task, purpose, and audience. **Writing 5.** With guidance and support from peers and adults, develop and strengthen writing as needed by planning, revising, editing, rewriting, or trying a new approach. **Writing 6.** With some guidance and support from adults, use technology, including the Internet, to produce and publish writing as well as to interact and collaborate with others; demonstrate sufficient command of keyboarding skills to type a minimum of two pages in a single sitting. **Writing 9.** Draw evidence from literary or informational texts to support analysis, reflection, and research.

STEP 1 Read Like a Writer

Review the key features of a persuasive essay listed below. Respond to any questions students might have.

Key Features of a Persuasive Essay
- Introduces the writer's claim about a topic
- Supports the claim with clear reasons and relevant evidence
- Clarifies the relationship among the claim, the reasons, and the evidence
- Maintains a formal style
- Provides a logical concluding statement, often urging the reader to agree with the writer

Choose a problem-solution or argumentative/persuasive text that students have already read to model key features. Display the model for students to see and point out each of the key features you have discussed.

STEP 2 Organize Your Ideas

Writing Prompt In the play *The Fabulous Perpetual Motion Machine,* a reporter comes to interview the Pérez twins about their invention. A real-life reporter interviews model-builder Garfield Minott in "A Model Scientist." State which interviewer better handles the interview and is therefore better able to gain insight about the subjects. Use details from both texts to develop your opinion.

Think Aloud Reread "A Model Scientist." Look at the kinds of questions the interviewer asks and the order in which they are asked. Notice how the interviewer begins with a question that sets the purpose of the interview: "What exactly do you do?" The questions that follow gather details about what and why Minott does what he does. Then, reread pp. 340–343 of *The Fabulous Perpetual Motion Machine* to review how Lee plans to conduct her interview and take photos. Make a list of the things the interviewer and the reporter say and do in order to gather information.

Guided Writing Help students use their lists and what they have learned from "A Model Scientist" to write their opinions. Explain that the first question always sets the purpose of an interview. Do the interviewers in both texts do this? Explain to students that they will begin their essays by clearly stating their opinion. The paragraphs that follow will use the facts and details gathered from the selections to persuade readers to agree with them. The essay should end with a concluding statement that restates the opinion and its supporting reasons.

STEP 3 Draft Your Writing

Have students use their lists and the model to write a persuasive essay. Remind them of the key features of a persuasive essay.

Think Aloud Begin by stating your opinion as clearly as possible. Be sure to link your opinion to reasons by providing facts and details that support your position. Your goal is to convince your readers to accept your opinion. Using persuasive words will help you do this.

Getting Started Tell students to begin writing their persuasive essays using their lists to keep them on track. Give them suggestions on where to place their facts and supporting details for best effect. Emphasize the importance of using correct grammar and complete sentences. Remind students to use a persuasive tone.

STEP 4 Evaluate Your Writing

Display the checklist below and have students use it to evaluate their persuasive essays. Circulate around the room and confer with individual students.

- ✓ Did I clearly state my opinion about which interview was handled better?
- ✓ Did I use facts, details, and explanations to support my opinion?
- ✓ Is my essay organized in a logical way?
- ✓ Did I use complete sentences and correct grammar?
- ✓ Did I use a persuasive tone?

Help students set goals and a plan for improving their writing as needed.

STEP 5 Revise and Publish

Help students follow through with their plans for revision. If time permits, have students trade interviews and offer suggestions for how to improve their writing.

Publishing Students can work with partners to turn their persuasive essays into radio commentaries. Record the commentaries.

Persuasive Essay

Objectives

- Identify the characteristics of a persuasive essay.
- Write a persuasive essay, using important facts and supporting details.
- Evaluate your writing.
- Revise and publish your writing.

Ⓒ Common Core State Standards

Writing 1. Write opinion pieces on topics or texts, supporting a point of view with reasons and information. **Writing 4.** Produce clear and coherent writing in which the development and organization are appropriate to task, purpose, and audience. **Writing 5.** With guidance and support from peers and adults, develop and strengthen writing as needed by planning, revising, editing, rewriting, or trying a new approach. **Writing 6.** With some guidance and support from adults, use technology, including the Internet, to produce and publish writing as well as to interact and collaborate with others; demonstrate sufficient command of keyboarding skills to type a minimum of two pages in a single sitting. **Writing 9.** Draw evidence from literary or informational texts to support analysis, reflection, and research.

STEP 1 Read Like a Writer

Review the key features of a persuasive essay listed below. Respond to any questions students might have.

Key Features of a Persuasive Essay

- Establishes a position by stating a claim, or opinion, about a topic
- Supports the claim with clear reasons and relevant evidence, demonstrating an understanding of the topic and the text
- Organizes the reasons and evidence in a clear and logical order, using persuasive words and phrases to support the claim
- Includes an introduction, body, and conclusion that follows from the argument presented
- Establishes and maintains a formal style

Choose a persuasive piece to model key features for students. Display the model for students to see and point out each of the key features you have discussed.

STEP 2 Organize Your Ideas

Writing Prompt Leonardo Da Vinci and Benjamin Waterhouse Hawkins each faced the task of sculpting a large statue of an animal. In preparation for the task, both took great care in studying the animal they wanted to sculpt. Write a persuasive essay in which you explain which sculptures you believe are better and why. Use details from both selections to support your claim.

Think Aloud A persuasive essay should convince your readers to accept your point of view. It should use persuasive words and phrases to support your claim. Before you begin writing, make a list of persuasive words and phrases to use in your essay. Think about the best way to present your opinion and which details to include from each selection to support your opinion.

Guided Writing Encourage students to use an outline to organize their essays. Display an outline as an example. Help students develop their outlines. Remind students that they should focus on details that will most effectively support their claims. Tell them to try to include at least two details for each point they make in their essays. Encourage students to use persuasive words and phrases.

STEP 3 Draft Your Writing

Have students use their lists or outlines to write their essays. Remind them of the key features of a persuasive essay.

Think Aloud Remember that persuasive essays should convince your readers of your point of view. Do not include information that will not support your opinion. Avoid repeating information. This will help keep your essay focused.

Getting Started Tell students to use their lists and outlines to begin writing their essays. Give them guidance on organization. Point out any places where they are including details that do not support their opinions. Remind students to use persuasive words and phrases to help convince their readers. Remind them to use correct grammar.

STEP 4 Evaluate Your Writing

Display the checklist below and have students use it to evaluate their essays. Circulate around the room and confer with individual students.

- ✓ Does all of the information in my essay support my opinion?
- ✓ Did I present the information in a logical order?
- ✓ Did I keep the essay focused and free of repeated information?
- ✓ Did I use persuasive words and phrases to help convince my readers?

Help students set goals and a plan for improving their writing as needed.

STEP 5 Revise and Publish

Help students follow through with their plans for revision. If time permits, have students trade essays and offer suggestions for improving the wording and illustrations.

Publishing Students can share their summaries with a partner or in a small group. Students should discuss the persuasive elements of each essay and how these help convince the reader.

Letter to the Editor

Objectives

- Identify the characteristics of a letter to the editor.
- Write a letter that uses persuasive language to convince your readers.
- Evaluate your writing.
- Revise and publish your writing.

© Common Core State Standards

Writing 1. Write opinion pieces on topics or texts, supporting a point of view with reasons and information. **Writing 4.** Produce clear and coherent writing in which the development and organization are appropriate to task, purpose, and audience. **Writing 5.** With guidance and support from peers and adults, develop and strengthen writing as needed by planning, revising, editing, rewriting, or trying a new approach. **Writing 9.** Draw evidence from literary or informational texts to support analysis, reflection, and research.

STEP 1 Read Like a Writer

Review the key features of a letter to the editor that are listed below. Respond to any questions students might have.

Key Features of a Letter to the Editor

- Is sent to the editor of a newspaper or magazine
- Is written in response to a story or article, an event, or an issue
- Usually aims to persuade others by supporting claims with clear reasons and relevant evidence
- Establishes and maintains correct formal letter format
- Provides a concluding statement related to the opinion

Choose a letter to the editor from a local newspaper or a magazine to model key features. Display the model for students to see and point out each of the key features you have discussed.

STEP 2 Organize Your Ideas

Writing Prompt Reread the poetry collection in Week 1 and the poems on pp. 162–165. Use specific details from the poems to write a letter to the editor of the local newspaper explaining why you believe poetry readings would benefit the community.

Think Aloud Remember that the goal of this letter is to convince readers that poetry readings would be good for the community. You want to interest people in the concept and provide details that will excite your readers about the event. Reread the poetry collections to find details about the poems that will make people want to come to or participate in a poetry reading.

Guided Writing Help students plan their letters. Suggest that they make a list of persuasive words and phrases they can use in their letters. Explain that they will begin their letters by providing details about poetry readings in order to create interest. They will conclude their letters by restating their opinions about why holding poetry readings is a good idea.

STEP 3 Draft Your Writing

Have students use their lists to write their letters. Remind them of the key features of a letter to the editor.

Think Aloud Remember that a letter to the editor is supposed to persuade readers to seriously consider your proposal. Be sure to include specific details about poetry readings. Don't forget to include an introduction to create interest and a conclusion that encourages people to attend poetry readings. Remember to use details from the poems to create interest.

Getting Started Tell students to use their lists to begin writing their letters. Give them guidance on creating an interesting introduction and a convincing conclusion. Emphasize the importance of using correct grammar and complete sentences in the introduction and conclusion. Point out any of the information in the body of the letter that needs clarification.

STEP 4 Evaluate Your Writing

Display the checklist below and have students use it to evaluate their letters. Circulate around the room and confer with individual students.

- ✓ Does my introduction use persuasive language?
- ✓ Did I clearly state specific reasons about why a community event such as this is important?
- ✓ Did I include details from the poems to support my opinion?
- ✓ Did I conclude the letter by restating my opinion?

Help students set goals and develop a plan for improving their writing as needed.

STEP 5 Revise and Publish

Help students follow through with their plans for revision. If time permits, have students trade letters and offer suggestions for improving their writing.

Publishing Students can discuss their letters with a partner or in small groups and focus on elements that make each letter convincing.

More Connect the Texts
Opinion

STEP 1 Read Like a Writer

Review the key features of an opinion listed below. Respond to any questions students might have.

Key Features of an Opinion

- Establishes an opinion by stating a claim, or position, about a topic
- Supports the claim with clear reasons and relevant evidence, demonstrating an understanding of the topic and the text
- Organizes the reasons and evidence in a clear and logical order, using persuasive words and phrases to support the opinion
- Includes an introduction, body, and conclusion that follows from the argument presented
- Establishes and maintains a formal style

Choose an opinion piece to model key features for students. Display the model for students to see and point out each of the key features you have discussed.

STEP 2 Organize Your Ideas

Writing Prompt *The Skunk Ladder* and *Journey to the Center of the Earth* both describe dramatic encounters with unpleasant animals. Briefly describe each encounter and then state your opinion about which animal you'd rather encounter. Support your opinion with details from each text.

Think Aloud Reread the passages about Mr. Muldoon's encounter with the skunk in *The Skunk Ladder* and Harry, Hans, and Professor von Hardwigg's encounter with the sea monsters in *Journey to the Center of the Earth.* Use a T-chart to takes notes about the two encounters. List information about *The Skunk Ladder* in one column and information about *Journey to the Center of the Earth* in the other column. Be sure to write down specific details that you will want to include in your opinion. Underline facts that you think deserve elaboration.

Guided Writing Help students use their T-charts to organize their writing. Tell them they will begin their opinions with a paragraph that introduces and briefly describes both encounters. They will then use one paragraph to state their opinions about which animal they'd rather encounter and why. They will conclude their opinion with a paragraph that restates their positions and convinces their readers.

STEP 3 Draft Your Writing

Have students use their T-charts to write their opinions. Remind them of the key features of an opinion.

Think Aloud Remember that your writing should convince readers of your opinion. Use persuasive language and precise words to describe each encounter and state your opinion. Try to make the reader see, hear, and smell the animals and experience the setting.

Getting Started Tell students to begin writing their opinions using their T-charts as a guide. Help them choose details to elaborate and persuasive language. Remind them to use correct grammar and include powerful adjectives.

STEP 4 Evaluate Your Writing

Display the checklist below and have students use it to evaluate their opinions. Circulate around the room and confer with individual students.

- ✓ Does my opinion use descriptive language and persuasive words and phrases?
- ✓ Is the writing organized in a logical way?
- ✓ Have I used powerful adjectives and precise words to create vivid images?
- ✓ Have I included a conclusion that restates my opinion about which animal I'd rather encounter?

Help students set goals and an improvement plan for their writing as needed.

STEP 5 Revise and Publish

Help students follow through with their plans for revision. If time permits, have students trade opinions and offer suggestions for how to improve their writing.

Publishing Students can use the computer to type their opinions. Post the finished opinions on a classroom or hallway bulletin board.

Persuasive Speech

Objectives

- Identify the characteristics of a persuasive speech.
- Write a speech, stating a claim and including supporting details, definitions, explanations, reasons, and examples.
- Evaluate your speech.
- Revise and deliver your speech.

Ⓒ Common Core State Standards

Writing 1. Write opinion pieces on topics or texts, supporting a point of view with reasons and information. **Writing 4.** Produce clear and coherent writing in which the development and organization are appropriate to task, purpose, and audience. **Writing 5.** With guidance and support from peers and adults, develop and strengthen writing as needed by planning, revising, editing, rewriting, or trying a new approach. **Writing 6.** With some guidance and support from adults, use technology, including the Internet, to produce and publish writing as well as to interact and collaborate with others; demonstrate sufficient command of keyboarding skills to type a minimum of two pages in a single sitting. **Writing 8.** Recall relevant information from experiences or gather relevant information from print and digital sources; summarize or paraphrase information in notes and finished work, and provide a list of sources. **Writing 9.** Draw evidence from literary or informational texts to support analysis, reflection, and research.

STEP 1 Read Like a Writer

Review the key features of a persuasive speech listed below. Respond to any questions students might have.

Key Features of a Persuasive Speech

- Meant to be formally presented to an audience
- Delivers a claim, or opinion, on an issue
- Has a main idea or thesis statement

Choose a persuasive speech that you can read to students to model key features. Display the model for students to see and point out each of the key features you have discussed.

STEP 2 Organize Your Ideas

Writing Prompt Adventurers are found in every time in history. Modern astronauts and the people who moved out West in the nineteenth century share a common trait—courage. Write a speech using the following claim: It takes courage to leave the security of home and venture into the unknown. Draw evidence from *Talk with an Astronaut, Ghost Towns of the American West,* and your own research to write the speech.

Think Aloud Writing a speech before you give it allows you time to think about what you want to say, organize the details, and practice the speech aloud without an audience. A persuasive speech focuses on a claim. Think about your claim. Reread the selections and make a list of details and examples that you can use in your speech as evidence to support your claim. Do additional research if you need to.

Guided Writing Encourage students to make an outline. Help them work in information from their list and organize the outline. Tell students that the first paragraph of their speech should introduce the claim in an interesting way. This will establish the purpose of the speech and grab the audience's interest. The introduction should be followed by several paragraphs, each with its own strong topic sentence. The topic sentences should be supported with concrete details, explanations, reasons, and examples. The speech should end with a strong concluding statement.

STEP 3 Draft Your Writing

Have students use their outlines to write their speeches. Remind them of the key features of a speech.

Think Aloud Remember that your speech will be heard. Use a variety of sentence types to create drama and to keep your listeners interested. Keep your audience and your purpose in mind. Choose words that are vivid and clear.

Getting Started Tell students to begin writing their speeches using their outlines to keep them on track. Give them suggestions on how to order their facts and supporting details. Emphasize the importance of using correct grammar, vivid words, and varied sentence structure. Remind them to end with a strong concluding statement.

STEP 4 Evaluate Your Writing

Display the checklist below and have students use it to evaluate their speeches. Circulate around the room and confer with individual students.

- ✓ Did I begin my speech with an interest grabber?
- ✓ Have I supported my claim with concrete details, explanations, reasons, and examples?
- ✓ Will my speech sound good when spoken?
- ✓ Have I used vivid words and varied sentence structures to maintain interest?
- ✓ Have I remembered my audience and my purpose?

Help students set goals and develop a plan for improving their speech as needed.

STEP 5 Revise and Publish

Help students follow through with their plans for revision. If time permits, have students trade speeches and offer suggestions for improving them.

Publishing Students can deliver their speeches in front of the class or make digital recordings to present to the class and their families.

How-to Article

Objectives

- Identify the characteristics of a how-to article.
- Write a how-to article that explains how to do something.
- Evaluate your writing.
- Revise and publish your writing.

© Common Core State Standards

Writing 2. Write informative/ explanatory texts to examine a topic and convey ideas and information clearly.
Writing 4. Produce clear and coherent writing in which the development and organization are appropriate to task, purpose, and audience.
Writing 5. With guidance and support from peers and adults, develop and strengthen writing as needed by planning, revising, editing, rewriting, or trying a new approach.
Writing 6. With some guidance and support from adults, use technology, including the Internet, to produce and publish writing as well as to interact and collaborate with others; demonstrate sufficient command of keyboarding skills to type a minimum of two pages in a single sitting.
Writing 9. Draw evidence from literary or informational texts to support analysis, reflection, and research.

STEP 1 Read Like a Writer

Review the key features of a how-to article that are listed below. Respond to any questions students might have.

Key Features of a How-to Article

- Uses a series of steps to explain a specific task or activity
- Provides all of the necessary steps
- Uses concrete details and clear, precise language to describe the steps
- Often uses time-order words such as *first, next,* and *last*
- Follows an appropriate and logically organized structure

Choose a how-to article that students have already read to model key features. Display the model for students to see and point out each of the key features you have discussed.

STEP 2 Organize Your Ideas

Writing Prompt Reread "All About Gymnastics" to gather advice on how to research a topic on the Internet. Then reread "Square Dancing" to find information that will help you develop search terms that you can use to conduct Internet research on how to do a specific square dance. Use the information you collect to write a how-to article that describes the steps in the dance.

Think Aloud Once you have conducted your research, you will need to organize the information into steps. How-to articles use steps because instructions are easier to follow if they are presented in a logical order. Use your research notes to make a list of the steps. Make sure that you do not leave out any of the steps. Think about how a diagram might help explain how to do the dance.

Guided Writing Help students use their lists to organize the information they have gathered into clear, easy-to-follow steps. Explain that they will begin their articles with two or three interesting sentences that tell about the square dance they will explain. They will then outline the steps in the body of the article. Encourage students to use time-order words or numbers to designate the steps. They will conclude their articles with a sentence or two that sum up why the square dance is enjoyable.

STEP 3 Draft Your Writing

Have students use their lists to write their how-to articles. Remind them of the key features of a how-to article.

Think Aloud Remember that a how-to article tells how to do something in easy-to-follow steps. Use clear, precise words so that your steps are easy to understand. Check to make sure that you have not left out any steps.

Getting Started Tell students to use their lists to begin writing their how-to articles. Give them guidance on organization and where diagrams might help. Point out any steps that are missing or unclear. Emphasize the importance of numbering the steps or using time-order words to indicate the steps in the process.

STEP 4 Evaluate Your Writing

Display the checklist below and have students use it to evaluate their articles. Circulate around the room and confer with individual students.

✓ Are my steps organized in the correct order?

✓ Did I leave out any steps?

✓ Did I use time-order transition words or numbers to help organize the steps?

✓ Did I use clear, precise words to make the steps easy to understand?

✓ Did I use diagrams to help the reader understand how to do the square dance?

✓ Does the article have an introduction and a concluding statement?

Help students set goals and develop a plan for making improvements to their writing where necessary.

STEP 5 Revise and Publish

Help students follow through with their plans for revision. If time permits, have students trade articles and offer suggestions for improving their writing.

Publishing Students can gather their how-to articles into a classroom book on square dancing.

More Connect the Texts
News Article

STEP 1 Read Like a Writer

Review the key features of a news article listed below. Respond to any questions students might have.

Key Features of a News Article

- Reports current events
- Has a headline, a byline, a lead, supporting details, and an ending
- Gives the most important information first as the lead
- Provides supporting evidence that includes facts, definitions, concrete details, quotations, and other information and examples
- Often includes text features, such as photos and captions

Choose a recent news article to model key features of the writing form. Display the model for students to see and point out each of the key features you have discussed.

STEP 2 Organize Your Ideas

Writing Prompt *The Unsinkable Wreck of the R.M.S.* Titanic and *Talk with an Astronaut* both discuss the use of technology. Write a newspaper article that describes for readers the importance of technology in learning about the wreck of the *Titanic* and in space exploration. Draw evidence for your newspaper article using specific details from the two selections.

Think Aloud A news article gives readers information and facts about an event. News articles usually provide information about who, what, where, and when. These are called the 4 Ws. You may want to use a 4 Ws chart to plan your article. Use the following headings for your chart: **What Happened, Who Was Affected, Where It Happened,** and **When It Happened.** Use your chart to collect information about the use of technology from both selections.

Guided Writing Help students complete their charts. Assist them in organizing the facts into the different categories. Explain that they will begin their news articles with a headline that describes the topic and will use their own name as a byline. They will then lead off with a strong introductory paragraph that includes the most important information. They will follow the lead paragraph with the body of the article, which will contain supporting details. Students will end their articles with a concluding statement.

STEP 3 Draft Your Writing

Have students use their charts to write their news articles. Remind them of the key features of a news article.

Think Aloud Remember that news articles begin with the lead—the most important information. You want to grab the reader's attention quickly. The body of the news article consists of supporting facts, details, and explanations. A concluding statement wraps up the article. Think about this organization as you write your article.

Getting Started Tell students to use their charts to begin writing their articles. Give them guidance on organization. Point out any places where they need more supporting details. Remind students that correct grammar and the use of transition words are important.

STEP 4 Evaluate Your Writing

Display the checklist below and have students use it to evaluate their news articles. Circulate around the room and confer with individual students.

- ✓ Is my article about a real event?
- ✓ Do I have a headline and a byline?
- ✓ Did I lead with my most important information?
- ✓ Did I include supporting sentences with facts, details, and explanations?
- ✓ Do I have a concluding statement?
- ✓ Did I use transition words to help with the flow of the article?

Help students set goals and a plan for improving their writing as needed.

STEP 5 Revise and Publish

Help students follow through with their plans for revision. If time permits, have students trade articles and offer suggestions for improving the writing.

Publishing Students can set up a class news blog and post their articles for friends and family members to read.

More Connect the Texts
Descriptive Essay

Objectives

- Identify the characteristics of a descriptive essay.
- Write a descriptive essay using facts and supporting details.
- Evaluate your writing.
- Revise and publish your writing.

© Common Core State Standards

Writing 2. Write informative/explanatory texts to examine a topic and convey ideas and information clearly. **Writing 4.** Produce clear and coherent writing in which the development and organization are appropriate to task, purpose, and audience. **Writing 5.** With guidance and support from peers and adults, develop and strengthen writing as needed by planning, revising, editing, rewriting, or trying a new approach. **Writing 6.** With some guidance and support from adults, use technology, including the Internet, to produce and publish writing as well as to interact and collaborate with others; demonstrate sufficient command of keyboarding skills to type a minimum of two pages in a single sitting. **Writing 8.** Recall relevant information from experiences or gather relevant information from print and digital sources; summarize or paraphrase information in notes and finished work, and provide a list of sources. **Writing 9.** Draw evidence from literary or informational texts to support analysis, reflection, and research.

STEP 1 Read Like a Writer

Review the key features of a descriptive essay listed below. Respond to any questions students might have.

Key Features of a Descriptive Essay
- Tells about real people, animals, things, and events
- Provides a description or an explanation of something
- Uses facts, definitions, concrete details, quotations, and clear, precise language to describe or explain
- Usually includes an introductory paragraph, several body paragraphs, and a concluding paragraph

Choose a descriptive essay that students have already read to model key features. Display the model for students to see and point out each of the key features you have discussed.

STEP 2 Organize Your Ideas

Writing Prompt: *The Truth About Austin's Amazing Bats* and "City Hawks" discuss Mexican Free-tailed bats and red-tailed hawks. Use evidence from the selections and additional Internet research to write a descriptive essay describing the characteristics of both animals.

Think Aloud Once you have collected details from the selections and from your Internet research, you will need to organize the information into an outline. Think about how best to organize the body of the essay. You want each paragraph to have a clear focus. Devoting one paragraph to each animal would a help accomplish this goal.

Guided Writing Help students organize their information and develop outlines. Explain that they will begin their essays by using the topic sentence in the first paragraph to establish the main idea. They will then use the two paragraphs in the body of the essay to describe the characteristics of each animal. They will end their essays with an effective closing paragraph and a list of sources.

STEP 3 Draft Your Writing

Have students use their outlines to write their descriptive essays. Remind them of the key features of a descriptive essay.

Think Aloud Remember that a descriptive essay is meant to give information. You should establish the main idea of the essay in the first paragraph. Each paragraph in the body of the essay should have a topic sentence to establish the paragraph's focus. The concluding paragraph should tie the essay together.

Getting Started Have students use their outlines to keep their writing on track. Check that students are devoting one body paragraph to Mexican free-tailed bats and one paragraph to red-tailed hawks. Check for topic sentences and for sufficient facts and details. Emphasize the importance of using correct grammar and complete sentences.

STEP 4 Evaluate Your Writing

Display the checklist below and have students use it to evaluate their compositions. Circulate around the room and confer with individual students.

- ✓ Does my essay have a logical organization?
- ✓ Does my introductory paragraph establish the main idea in a topic sentence?
- ✓ Are the main ideas in my body paragraphs supported by facts and details?
- ✓ Do I have an effective closing paragraph?
- ✓ Have I used clear, precise words so that my descriptions are easy to understand?

Help students set goals and a plan for improving their writing as needed.

STEP 5 Revise and Publish

Help students follow through with their plans for revision. If time permits, have students trade compositions and offer suggestions for improving their writing.

Publishing Students can e-mail their essays to family and friends.